UNSTOPPABLE

YOUR SELF DEVELOPMENT JOURNEY SIMPLIFIED

KSHITIJA AHIRE & ROHAN GHARATE

Made with ♥ on the Notion Press Platform
www.notionpress.com

To

Lord MAHADEV

For Bringing

Love, Prosperity, Wealth, Health, Power, Fame, and massive professional and Spiritual Success

in the life of the Reader of this book- UNSTOPPABLE

It is important to read the "foreword" before starting the book

ꕥ

Contents

Title Page vii

From The Author's Desk ix

Preface xi

Acknowledgements xiii

1. Advice For 20-year-old 1
2. Things To Do Before 30 17
3. 13 Hacks To Save Money 33
4. Selfish Tips For Better Life 51
5. Distract From Distraction 67
6. Harsh Truth Of Relationships 84
7. 7 Wonderful Habits 92
8. Mind's Seven Tricks 103
9. Spirituality : A Lively Part Of Life 123
10. Tools To Become Unstoppable 132

Congratulations 143

Title Page

UNSTOPPABLE

Your Self-Development Journey Simplified

Kshitija Ahire & Rohan Gharate

From The Author's Desk

You may start reading this book only if you are committed to changing your life. It is a shame for this book if the reader is comfortable with his/her messy and cheap life. The book asks for pure game changers with a burning desire to change their lives and the world to achieve the goal. **The reader should not be a customer of this book, who will analyze and generate a pros-cons review about this book.** This book will help the people keen to become an asset to this beautiful world and surrender themselves to this book and follow all the principles for the entire year and see the positive results. **The book is not solely a motivational book, but a practical book that demands both your mental and physical engagement.**

We challenge and suggest the readers to complete the book within one month. Please read the book everyday and follow it every day for a year to witness changes. **To maximize the benefits, be in touch with the authors of this book on the provided handles. Get solutions for your problems and participate in their events.** The tools for some of the practices mentioned in the book are in the 10th chapter. Therefore, **you may go to the 10th chapter and read it whenever you need. It is a bonus chapter.**

It is a warning that while following the book, you will face the pain due the transformation happening in you. **You decide, if to take the pain of hardwork or the pain of embarrassment and regret, and work accordingly.**

As per the discipline of the universe, one needs to acknowledge the thing to get the utmost benefit out of it. So, make sure you aknowledge the book and be grateful for its presence in your life

PREFACE

I sincerely appreciate everyone who took the time to read this book. So what is "UNSTOPPABLE" really about? You must have felt the fire within you as you read the name. Everyone, regardless of wealth or poverty, experiences issues throughout life, But the true human is the one who never stops crying and punches the difficulties back with power and courage within himself/herself.

You are "UNSTOPPABLE," which implies that nothing is impossibly difficult in life if you are dedicated and focused on what you want to do, and nobody can hold you back or drag you down. No matter how severe the issues are, there is always a solution; all we need to do is know about it. Here, Unstoppable is your solution. When I was younger, I used to scream and cry in a corner of one room whenever a difficulty entered my life. However, as I got older, I started reading books and attending webinars, which showed me that although life might be difficult at times, one should always respond positively to it by carrying out the action and this book will help you to get motivated and will teach you values and discipline. However, this book will teach you a lot of stuff that you might not know. This book was written with a lot of motivation with the help of many philosophies, psychologies, and real-life experiences. It will enlighten you of the truth and the facts of which you were unaware.

How unstoppable was made? As a result of our extensive discussion, we discovered that many individuals in society are unaware of the facts we have provided in this book, which will undoubtedly help you develop personally and broaden your knowledge and abilities. This book will assist you with guidance for the 20s, money-saving tips, relationships, and inspiring stories. However, the knowledge we shared in this will help you grow your life with peaceful and high vibrations. When you read positive things, positive things happen to you. You will be getting some techniques to practice daily and will help you to make it a routine. This book will always help you to find yourself and will encourage you. “UNSTOPPABLE” comes with Most of my own reflections, my own observations, and my own experiences.

We used to play a game called book cricket in school. where the score on each "ball" was determined by the page number after selecting a random page from a book. Since we don’t score runs in book cricket, I picture this book as one of those games. Instead, here we are reminded, we put words to our thoughts and we become more aware. Every day, open a chapter.

Read one, maybe three pages. Reflect upon them. Maybe make some notes. Or just smile at how it made you feel. We’ve given you certain tasks and challenges, and I implore you to complete them so you may get to know yourself better. We wrote “UNSTOPPABLE” with a lot of inspiration in it to help you become more conscious of who you are, what you think, and what your vision and life’s purpose are! Take care to underline key passages in the book once you’ve finished reading it so you may refer back to it whenever you like. I strongly recommend you finish this book in one go and avoid taking breaks of many days and imply in your life. I'm hoping this book will be a great resource for you in all circumstances and will help your career and passion flourish.

-Kshitija Ahire & Rohan Gharate

Acknowledgements

We as authors acknowledge our parents for their support and teachings.

We are thankful to our online and offline mentors for sharing their immense ocean OF knowledge.

We are grateful to all the offline and online resources to allow us gather authentic information for our readers.

We are so thankful to our readers to give a big pleasure to this book by allowing it to become one of the reasons for your ultimate success and fulfilled life.

Finally, we as authors are thankful to ourselves to make this valuable and life changing information to the people of this beautiful planet and one of of the most evolved species in the universe.

I

Advice For 20-Year-Old

Everyone has limitless potential

Born in the same hospital, Harry and Shyam cried upon witnessing the detachment from their Mothers' wombs. They were happy and laughed together. They shade out the same tears. They ate the same first meal, They played with the same toys, and their age and personalities matched too. Yet, 30 years later, Harry grew up to be an elite soccer player. While Shyam ended up attending a prestigious college and completing his degree in physics. I wonder, what might have gone differently. The difference is created by values, decisions, inspiration, and discipline. The difference is created by the way of being UNSTOPPABLE. Every person keeps the potential of becoming wealthy. The sky is not the limit, either. If each person developed the necessary belief system, skills, and work ethic within themselves, they could accomplish great things.

If you make the decision to accomplish your goal, nothing is out of your reach! You just need to be ready to pay "what it takes." You must have "**the right stuff**" within you. If we allowed our current potential to decide our future triumphs, nothing innovative or challenging could be accomplished. The potential of people rises as we consistently work toward our goals, human potential is boundless.

It is scribbled in history that believer makes reality bend. Believe in your goal, and imagine it to be already achieved. Believe yourself to be already possessing that first million, that first Ferrari, that huge mansion. We are made up of that same element that makes up the stars and the entire universe. Our body performs the same task that the universe performs on a bigger scale. The realization of this truth opened the doors of multiple possibilities and extraordinary achievements. This is the same belief that you need to think about while meditating. Close your eyes with a deep breath, imagining your oneness with the universe. Your oneness with the Shiva. Your oneness with infinite potential is stored in this huge universe and is available for use whenever needed.

Set your POTENTIAL in accordance with your goal, not your Goal in accordance with your potential.

Get out of your comfort zone

Success is a never-ending process. It comes to those with a growth mentality. Growth is what keeps you out of your comfort zone. The stale life that can be described as the stationary water in a pond is called life in a comfort zone. Who is responsible to take it into a comfort zone? It is the soul with forgotten dreams and immense inner potential. Scrolling reels all day, spending parent's money without any intention of compound multiplication, and staring at a girl without any intention of literally asking her out are the habits of cowards. Cowards are meant to stay in their own rooms instead of going out with a plan of conquering the house and the world. Moving out of your comfort zone is a signature of energy flow and the best thing is **where the energy flows attention goes**. It is extremely easy to detect if you are out of your comfort zone or into it. Sit quietly with all distractions away, look at your life and ask these questions to yourself.

1. Did I get any public attention for a bigger impact on society?
2. Did I earn any extra cash by serving people in an impactful way?
3. Am I causing any movement in my life?

If the answer to these questions is NO, then you need to make changes. You need to get up from your bed and sit on that rusted table, not used in a while and build something for yourself, for your family, and for your mental and physical surroundings. If the answer to these questions is YES, then you are doing great. Keep it up! Just level up a bit now. Remember, **the principle of being unstoppable is having a growth mindset and leveling up every next move**. The master tip of constant growth is constant learning. You need to know that you know nothing. You need to build yourself to build a dreamland around. We will talk about this ahead in the book.

Why not be in a comfort zone? If you remain in your comfort zone, you would lose many excellent chances for growth. What you are capable of you will never know. The sea is not entirely visible from the shore, but sea exploration reveals a wealth of information. Multiple shores, indeed! When you eventually push yourself, overcome your fear, and accept the changes taking place, you will realize your worth. Do good deeds, they advise. Do bad things as well! Life is an adventure! Do anything. Just show some energy, and make your mark goodness or badness does not matter. What matters the most is your goal. **The goal is universally good else all is bad.** And this will support your development.

There used to be numerous small flowers among the large ones in a beautiful garden. There was a tiny flower—or should I say, a neglected flower—in one of the corners. Everyone would admire the flowers like roses, lilies, etc., thus no one would notice or care. The tiny flower used to be extremely anxious. He once criticized God for his appearance and asked him to make him a rose. He ignored the advice of other flowers to stay as he was. He observed the greatness of other roses up close and wanted to feel the same, therefore he would do anything to be a rose. Finally, God complied with his request and changed him into a rose. Now that he had changed into a rose, everyone loved him. He was now really content with his new appearance. He was enjoying the praise of others. There was a powerful wind one day. The powerful wind blew away all the flowers, especially the large ones. There were several blossoming plants uprooted. The little ones crept into the bushes and hid. The breeze carried the changed rose away. He was on his way out. The other tiny flowers were laughing at him as he took his final breaths. They mocked him and reminded him of their instructions. The rose said, "I am not sorry for losing my life, but I am pleased that I am dying as a rose, not a neglected one," and he didn't seem to mind. "I shall pass away satisfied as well as at peace. I am proud that I decided to change, I decided to go out into the world and pay the price it required. I transformed, I changed." With these words, he rested in true peace and pride.

The comfort zone is the enemy of achievement; by escaping it and embracing life's challenges, you will lead a successful life. We never feel at ease in our comfort zone. A ship can be found at the shore, but it was designed to sail through the waves, not to remain there. Put a lot of effort into succeeding.

Step outside your comfort zone to reach success!

Getting out of your comfort zone means:

- Leaving your comfort zone entails challenging yourself, trying new things, and doing everything differently.
- Learn new things and broaden your skill set in the workplace.
- Try out different creative activities.
- Visit new locations while you travel.
- Question your beliefs, debate new beliefs and follow those stays.
- Make a mental and physical shift for your betterment towards your aim.
- Give yourself a deadline, and shift your speed to a greater number; enlarge your energy flow.

Leave your place to go for a higher one

"Universe takes up the small to give the big." I bet all of you are aware of this phrase. Matter neither be created nor be destroyed is true for eternity. Even in the case of the universal business, we need to give one thing up to take up the other. That is better known as the price you pay to create the reality you desire. Additionally, society does not define greatness, you do. Someone can even be ready to give up his/her job at NASA to just be a math teacher at a government school. When you explore new ideas and step outside your comfort zone, you learn that leaving your current location is necessary if you wish to ascend to a higher level.

Nobody can stop you once you decide to move on for yourself. I visited a friend of mine one weekend. It seemed a great opportunity she seized at such a young age. Congratulating her was a compulsion for the commendable personality she built for a highly valued opportunity. However, the scene was nowhere as I expected it to be. A vibe of instability and boredom grabbed me as I entered her apartment. Messy bed with an awful odor of stagnant water. Her house was not meant to be this at all. She was a well-deserving highly respected girl among her peers. Upon asking she said, "my mental health is on holiday with a constant decline in physical and social health." "The job pressure and work load are killing me," she said; "I do perform the best among all and they are always ready to give me a higher paycheck and I even ask for it," she added in desperation. Listening to her cry, I was sure that she is missing an important part of her life, but as this job is highly valued in her and her parents' view she cannot dare to leave it. Yet, this was the decision she needed to make to release herself from the hell of depression and loneliness. I emphasized the value of moving on from one place to another in order to succeed. Rewired her mind and destroyed the blockage of certainty in her mind through the lessons mentioned in this very book. And look! A few days later, there she is at my door steps to thank me for this life-changing advice. She immediately landed the best position with more money and in a fantastic location. Well, some tricks of the Law of Attraction and Law of Vibration were involved too. Now, no one can stop her from achieving rich yet peaceful life. She is, now, unstoppable! In order to obtain the finest one, you must make a sacrifice. However, she is a person who lives with the discipline of accepting whatever the universe gives. If you keep on rereading, you won't be able to begin your new chapter in life.

It should also be kept in mind that the human power that dares to manage the universe shall be ready for extreme sacrifices. The universe gives us what it has planned for us, however, some brave individuals tend to bend reality according to them. Let me introduce you to one of my colleagues- Jay. Jay has seen the loneliness and bullying from the closest. He had planned all of his life and his achievement and is a keen believer in the Law of Attraction(LOA) with a great understanding of it. He believes- "there are people who, in their early 20s realize that the universe, actually, works their way. But, only a few of them survive the heavy tests of the universe that tries to mold them and the rest live by the phrase- 'I am thrilled to have an unplanned life and accept whatever the universe has to offer.'" In spirituality, such people of the great threshold of acceptance are slaves of the Maya and tend to make their lives better by exposing their feminine part to the Maya and worshiping her. Maya is called Stri (Feminine). While the few people who pass the tests of the universe find every possible way to get to what they want not what the universe gives. They are stubborn children who are not happy with the greatest toys in the world but demand the mother as it is all that child wants. Such people have more clear goals; instead of wanting a job, they demand a specific position in a specific job. Such people are worriers that fight the Maya to snatch what they wanted. Such people are worshipers of Purusha (Masculine). Now, many of you are this kind of person even I am. Nevertheless, I remember that one time I realized the cost of being a masculine worshiper through Jay. Continuing his story of loneliness and bullying, one detail that should be considered is that he was unaffected by it because he was tolerating all of it for his aim. His goal was his god. It was as if he is controlling the reality we all live in. The time arrived; ages were aging, and time was calling upon different possibilities of Jay's destiny. But, the intellect of LOA and the law of vibration could not be impelled to surrender. He applied all of his hard work to get into the university of his dreams as it would be the last step to get into CERN (Conseil Européen pour la Recherche Nucléaire", or European Council for Nuclear Research). Completing his degree in particle physics was easy, but getting into the university was difficult. Getting into The University for Classical and Quantum Physics would be his direct ticket to CERN. He put in all his work ethic to do what he could. The things that are out of reality had to be attracted through the power of the mind and universal connection. In the most focused and blissful state, it was unexpected to witness a tragedy that would open a door to a new understanding of reality creation. Jay lost his father. In a certain path of emotional reaction, it was expected for Jay to sob and halt his journey to take care of his family. But, unintroduced to the cost of his demand, he prepared himself to pay whatever it takes. He was unmoved by the crises in his life. The death of a loved one could not bring tears into his eyes because 'he was admitted to The University for Classical and Quantum Physics' the previous day. He experienced the neutrality of mixed emotions of happiness and sorrow and silence of enlightenment of a new thought.

People, the point is that, if the universe gives you something it takes the thing that you are capable of giving thus you should let it go. But, If you create a reality that is higher for you, you never know what the universe will take thus detach yourself from all that you have and focus on your aim- the reality that you create for yourself and the world.

Think yourself in the right direction and do mastery by taking the right steps

The work is done inside of your mind. Unavoidable outcomes are created when our thoughts reach our subconscious minds. "Subconscious creates reality." Your memory contains both good and bad experiences. As a result, you get both negative and positive ideas. It is important to teach your brain to filter out unfavourable thoughts and cultivate optimistic thinking. For this, We must always exercise mental discipline. Optimistic thinking looks like an age-old formula of saying and motivating. But, a deep study proves that optimism comes into a high vibrational state. It connects the dots to the Law of Vibration which states- "The higher the vibration, the more the chance of the desired result." Most people fail to use the Law of Attraction correctly because they miss the part where it is 'Viberation's problem. I recommended one of my colleague's research on the Law of Vibration and apply it to the Law of attraction. And it did work every time. Thus, I recommend you too to do the same while moving ahead in the journey of becoming unstoppable.

1. Learn to say "No"

Think of a time when just saying "NO" kept you out of every trouble. No and negation pops out in every aspect of our life. It is inevitable to consider its importance when we see that the basis of our life is decision making and the basis of decision-making is saying Yes or No. However, 'yes' has been an overrated player in the game of decisions due to this 'be-good' syndrome society is suffering through. So, it is truly important to embrace the negation in life as Yes, most of the time, makes you stoppable.

Our minds are constantly filled with a variety of ideas, not all of which are uplifting. If they come, they will force you to do undesirable things, so before you become comfortable, say "No." It will help you think more logically and prevent unwelcome thoughts in their paths. "No" opens the possibility of truth while Yes closes every possibility of information you should be open to. As we all know the place that is full of possibilities is eternally the most energetic. That is why scriptures respect and embrace 'No or nothing' more than 'Yes or something.' You may even say no to every decision that you take for your peers because later you may say yes. But, a No after Yes is said to be a symbol of cowardness and incapability. Thus, learn to say No and stop for a better decision instead of flowing into the environment's or any person's pressure.

1. Take control of your thought with deep breathing.

You must be aware of and grateful for your breath if you wish to control your thought for desired results. Free things lose their value, according to a proverb. Humans are quite skilled at taking things for granted, it is a truth. You can, however, modify this for your benefit. Today, recognize the power of your breath because it is the main tool for achieving liberation and enlightenment. You may assume that this is all nonsense. However, I must suggest you to believe your own research. It is after short research that you will understand the true meaning of breathing. All of these things will then make more sense. For now, just perform this one process to control your thought with the help of your breath.

Assume you got a thought- 'X'. This thought is making you feel insecure or sad or something you don't want to feel. So, firstly embrace the thought X. Second, decide the thought you want to replace X with. Let us say, it is the thought- 'Y'. Third, take a few deep breaths and breathe a little faster. In through the nose, out through the mouth. Breathe really deep. Fill your stomach, then chest then shoulders up and reverse the process while exhaling. Shoulders down, chest in, stomach in. Repeat this breathing 10 to 20 times with a focus on breaths. Fourth, exhale the last breath and hold it there until you are out of breath. In the meantime, visualize Y thought in front of you. Make that thought clear. Now, when you feel, breathe in rapidly taking that Y thought into your body, and hold your breath again for 15 seconds approximately. In the meantime, imagine that Y thought nourishing every cell of your body and don't think about X thought at all. It is lost now. After 15 seconds, breath out and stay normal. Try to feel the positivity and desirable feeling of Y thought in your mind and body.

And this is how you may control your big disappointing thought. And for small undesired thoughts, just take one deep breath and take your mind to some work or other thought. Here, the power of distraction really pays off!

3. Keep a journal.

Do you know the reason for my love of keeping a daily journal? Why do I only have a small circle of friends? Why do I like to be among close friends only? I was once listening to a podcast when the line "we should always write our own journal" caught my attention. I decided I should go through this. I simply began writing about my everyday adventure that night. And I started using it to communicate my feelings. I used to write things into it that I could not share with anyone else. I found that keeping a daily notebook improved my awareness, brain wiring, and self-love. I found a friend there with whom I can share my joy and sorrow. Even reading about my previous days taught me a lot, which enabled me to correct my faults. The more you journal the more you are aware of your behavior and your thought patterns and the more subsequently you will get to know what changes you have to make for your growth.

"Fill your paper with the breathings of your heart". When you keep a journal and write daily what all kinds of stuff you did you will get to analyze things. Laying down your thoughts and your goals on a piece of paper is making a blueprint for your construction. And, you know, Blueprint is the path towards an accurate and unstoppable construction. Almost every successful people believes in writing a journal.

Journal is the only friend with whom you share your life in the most transparent way. And, **transparency is the easiest way to be**

truthful. Writing a journal helps you to gain self-confidence and improve your writing and communication skills and also to reduce stress and anxiety. This makes you enough for yourself, so you don't depend on others to get you improved.

Make a separate book and start writing today. It is better today because tomorrow never comes. C'mon!!! grab up and start writing from today night.

- Put a date at the top of the book and then start writing.
- Start by blowing your present day's to-do list.
- You may write what you did during your entire day.
- What thoughts did you think?
- What are your goals?
- And what do you need to make changes in yourself and how can you grow?
- You may write gratitude for today and your loved ones.
- And, finally, put tomorrow's date and make your to-do list for the next day. (Don't make a to-do list your motivation, Make it a discipline. Completing a to-do list is a DISCIPLINE.)
- My personal opinion would be to draw about your goal in your journal too. Drawing makes your mind visualize and **"Visualization is the prominent way to make the universe work for you**!"

4. Shift your perspective, shift your paradigm.

Life is all about how your perspective is !! it is all about how you look at things and not how they are in themself. When you cultivate good thoughts and see from a positive perspective things will fall into place. For example:- If you are a painter and you painted a mountain it is upon you how you look at it like a mountain or a molehill.

In her tenth grade, Jane struggled academically and was scared of algebra. She became anxious and started crying the night before her mathematics exam because she felt she was unable to tackle the problems. When her sister addressed her crying, she quickly inquired. Her explanation followed. "You just go and take the test and your hard work will pay off," her sister then stated. If you keep thinking negatively, it will eventually enter your subconscious mind and cause you more problems than expected. Marks don't determine your future; you do. Simply stated, it requires a better perspective. Perspective plays a better role when you are building your reality. When an aeroplane is just an idea, many critics objected and disqualified it. It was a reality that was not in the physicality, but it was only that perspective that kept the desire in many thinkers alive and we got an Air-way transport system.

If you are feeling weak or discouraged you just have to reframe your mindset and change that feeling into energy. Your brain is very much like a bank every day you make a thought and deposit it in your "mind bank" these thoughts deposit and grow into memory when you settle down to think or when you face a problem, in effect, you say to your memory bank. This memory bank, in turn, goes into your subconscious realm and becomes your reality. So you see, the thoughts you deposit now will give outcomes in the future. You may even think of it as an investment that you do right from the time sperm and egg turns into a fetus.

If you think in an optimistic way in each situation then it will happen in that way only. Perspective can cause two people to look differently at the same thing and grab the results accordingly. "Your perspective can either become your prison or your passport". See failures as opportunities, not as obstacles. **Focus on the positive, instead of negative**. However, some people get power through the negatives too. Anger turns out to be a friend for most people than a foe. So, if it is the case, no one has any problem with that too. After all, the primary goal is to use the energy at its max to achieve our goals smoothly.

I. Deposit your positive thoughts in your memory bank.
II. Confident, successful people do not give it another thought they specialize in converting any thought into getting "desired"

results.

III. When you are alone with your thoughts -when you are driving your car or eating alone- recall pleasant, positive experiences. Put good thoughts in your memory bank. This will help you to boost your confidence and will give you an "I-sure-feel-good" feeling. It helps to keep your body functioning right, too.

IV. Just before you go to sleep think about good thoughts in your memory bank. Focus on your goal, visualize it, and feel it completed. Count your blessings. Recall the many good things you have to be thankful for your partner, your children, your friends, your health, and your goal getting completed regardless of its completion status. Recall all the good things you saw people do today. Recall your all victories and accomplishments. Go over the reasons why you are glad to be alive.

V. Destroy all negative(undesired) thoughts before they become mental monsters

Embrace all of the gifts of your life – and live FEARLESSLY. **Fearlessness is the way to becoming Unstoppable.**

Where focus goes energy flows

After a long time, Jack and Jill reunited. Jill was astounded by Jack's development over these years. She addressed him with many questions. Jill asks, "how have you undergone so many changes, whether they were for personal or spiritual growth? Your achievements seem to be unique." Jack answered "I never focused on getting good grades as a child but rather on being the center of attention and deserving of recognition. I always had a specific outlook on my achievements and tried to get what really will help me in life rather than short-term satisfaction. One of the things is that I used to imagine myself on a stage with enormous respect, and a vision for the future. Today, all of that is coming true."

Jack was successful as he achieved what he wanted. The part in the spotlight is the way he saved a massive amount of energy on meaningless acts and put that into objects that truly seemed meaningful to him. Through his thoughts and through his actions, the energy was always flowing towards his short-term aim and now he has achieved it. That is the secret- "where FOCUS goes ENERGY flows."

When you nourish your thoughts then that thought expands if you want to get 100000 lakhs per month then you will think about it.

wherever you go or you will manifest this thing and one day surely you will achieve your goal. The more you get your focus on the stuff that things eventually expand. The correct way to visualize it is to use the Law of Assumption. With the law of vibration, the law of assumption plays an equal role in directing your energy to your desired state and attracting it. It is foolish to say- "I will have 10 crores by next month." Instead, say and assume- "I am experiencing the richness and am delighted to have my first 10 crores." Feel that emotion you added to your goal as you assume to have already achieved your goal. This is the way toward unstoppable manifestation

When you think you want the best university and you manifest it then you will surely get it. In simple words, **your life is controlled by what you think**, and feel., radiate when you give enough amount of energy to something, you become one with it and people around you start to see you in that place, they feel you in that state and this how the reality is created. The best examples are sadhus. Take aghoris, for instance, they offer extreme energy to one idea of Shiva that they unify with that state and people start to see shiva in them. So, they eventually achieve that desired state. They became a shiva-yogi. So you need to think, feel, and radiate the state you want not that you do not. **Whatever you focus on expands and intensifies.**

What we feel is the result of what we choose to think. When a person thinks and focuses on saying that "I am not happy in this job. I am poor. I don't have a car". Then this thinking of that person will get power over the mind and this thing will happen.

Think, doubt, and fail; Think, believe, and succeed.

A person is a producer of his own thoughts. Believe big and grow big.

When you start to believe in yourself then eventually good things do start to happen.

- Think "success", and "don't think failure."
- Think "I will win" not "probably will lose."
- I am the "best" and not I am outclassed.
- "I can do" it never "I cannot."
- "I am to be successful" and not "I am unsuccessful."

Compare yourself to yourself

Everyone asks themselves, "How can we evolve as people?" How can we become powerful? I recently saw the perfect illustration of this question yesterday while attending a family event. Tina, my cousin, came, and everyone was delighted at how she looked. I went to her and questioned how she maintained such a lovely beauty, how she became spiritual, and from where she obtained her confidence. In response, she revealed that in the lockdown of 2020-2021, when she was by herself and alone, she realized that things should change. She was self-conscious, but she made a deliberate effort to avoid comparing herself to others and instead compared her current self with the one that was or will be better than now. She saw her desired state. She focused on the well-being of her body and her pleasure. Her daily practice of yoga and meditation helped her become more self-aware and enhanced her worth. According to her, **comparing yourself to yourself will ultimately improve you as a person and bring you happiness**, however, comparing yourself to others will always cause jealousy.

See yourself where I was and how I am today. Remind yourself of the good in you. Day by day what you do is who you become. If I can reach here in 10 days then imagine after 10 years where I can reach!

Compare yourself to what I was, what I am, and what I am going to be.

Comparing yourself to yourself is a good habit. When you see yourself in past years you will get to know what improvements you need to do in yourself. You will realize what mistakes you did and will get the best of yourself from it.

Task: Make a list of things which you regret you did and think how you can correct them and you surely will feel best.

Often, twenties is hard where you go to college and, meet friends, face peer pressure, family pressure, etc. we all are going through so many transitions in our twenties

Looking back on where we came from, the challenges we've faced, and the goals we've reached over the years has been a very big part of our personal growth in our twenties. it often reflects on how we thought and behaved during our teen years.

When we compare ourselves we often sense jealousy. but comparing yourselves with your previous self can motivate you to get big and achieve what you want. Look at your inner self and love you what are and think about how successful you are going to be.

Mistakes help you to learn and teach you. They are the teachers of our life.

No matter how was the past version of yours, you should be proud of yourself because you decided to strive to be the better person, you are today.

II

Things To Do Before 30

Travel solo for 30 days

"Real experience always has a better value." Just picture yourself on a lone trip, making your way to your destination. An incredible traveling experience. Water dripping down the mountain peaks. You cannot see what is ahead as the thick fog obscures the entire route. Monkeys linger around while lions roar in the distant forests. The chilly wind twirling reminds you of the changed region. Sitting on a hilltop watching the sunrise while You are receiving a ray of morning sunshine and witnessing flowers dance. Even just imagining it is fantastic, right? Traveling alone will provide you with this fascinating scenery and experience. With this, come some dreadful experiences as well. That lonely night and sleeping on footpaths. Taking care of your single bag and managing a place to clean yourself up. Every time I plan on going on a solo trip without any money and luggage, I only think of the bathroom. Where will

I get to clean myself up? But, it is such an adventurous journey that teaches you to manage yourself even when the resources are not available. These treks make you mature and turn you into a better version of yourself with respect to your body and mind. Every time you step back and reflect on your life's years, it is common to think back on the past and remember happy and sad occasions, novel encounters, sweet and sour festivals, perplexing questions, and intriguing enlightenment. Such moments surely do get into your front head when you are alone, and your body is in motion while trying hard to survive. This gives you an insight into yourself and the world.

- **It is a contemporary learning experience.**

I visited Shiva's residence once. Seeing him unpacking his bags, I asked- "Where are you returning from?". He went on to describe his lengthy, six-day solo expedition to "Kedarnath." He was overjoyed to share with me his encounters with meeting new individuals. How he spent his time in a one-room cabin and taking steam baths in Gauri Kund. "Bhang ki Chutney" is a particularly special cuisine from the Pahari region of Uttarakhand and Kedarnath, and he ate it in the local dhaba. This obviously added a new flavor to a new dish to his mouth. "I ascended the mountain of over 14 kilometers" he added in a proud tone. He said that he was almost suffocating and with no one to back him up it was a work of great valor to cross the place as soon as possible. Alone as he WALKED, he took some shortcuts through dense forests among the chirping of crickets, barking of wild dogs, howling of wolfs, roaring of lions, grunting of pigeons, and many more. He was not even able to recall all the sounds but the nights he spends in the forest felt like an eternity. "Forest has its own aura with an amazing sound the forest makes altogether" he exclaimed. Finally, through his thrilling journey through the jungle of trees and buildings, he reached his destination. It was the calmness never felt before. "It was the bliss of hard-earned aim" he describes. The temple, to him, was perfect for his daily meditation practice. He came across a sadhu who was performing the mantra Japa while dressed in an orange robe as a symbol of supreme sacrifice in the search for higher truth. Shiva and sadhu went deep into a discussion about their spiritual journey and certain sadhanas. He described how he took sannyasa, left his life and family, and lived in caves in the Himalayas before coming here to see Mahadev and receive his blessings. Also, how the sadhu lived on a magnificent mountain covered in vegetation and filled with good energy, and he came to Kedarnath where everyone came to visit Lord Shiva and ask for his blessings. He described everything perfectly, but the knowledge he received was left untouched. "You need to experience it yourself," he said "What I learned throughout my expedition is the part of Param-Gyan (supreme knowledge)" he added with tears of ecstasy in his eyes.

The conclusion is that you will learn about other cultures' ways of speaking, eating, and traveling as you visit various locations. And the knowledge you get is just indescribable with the language of limited words and expressions. Doing this will encourage you to step outside of your comfort zone and teach you to appreciate what you already have.

Things never stop at whatever age you are. there is no age limit or boundary specific to learning new things. 81-year-old male Lev Sarkisov, like most of the others on this list, established the record for climbing Mount Everest at the time as the oldest man to do so. Sarkisov, a Georgian with Armenian ancestry, conquered Mount Everest in 1999, albeit his record has undoubtedly been surpassed since then. But Sarkisov is the oldest Armenian to have ever scaled the mythical summit. "The decision to fly the Armenian flag was extremely risky" Sarkisov admitted. He began his ascent of Everest in the morning and remained there until rough sunset. "I made the flag at the hotel using cloth that I purchased in Bayazet in three different colors" he informed. Even at this young age, he scaled Mount Everest, 8,849 meters high.

Traveling is just an adventure from where you can learn. You can probably travel at any age but traveling specifically in your 30 s is completely another experience you can get in your life. Moreover, It equips you with skillset to achieve your dream at a young age when you have the power and ability to tolerate such hardships.

- Meet people, make connections
- Observe and improve your capability
- Address the kindness and cruelty of the world
- Understand human and nature's behavior
- Know different cultures and rituals
- Strengthen your spiritual aura, Make it more adaptive
- Enlighten yourself in loneliness

"Travel the world with only 1 bag"

Go solo Go far!

Traveling alone will enable you to have a variety of these experiences, which will make you realize how wonderful your life is. You will become a more mature and humble person as a result. You will come to understand your value as a person. You will become aware of your obligations if you stay by yourself and are isolated. Tara my school friend had put scuba diving on his bucket list, and after a long wait, she finally got the chance to do it. The oxygen cylinder on her back provided her with oxygen as she dove deep into the ocean. As she continued to descend, she observed numerous little fish with brilliantly colored fins. She heard the water, and those five minutes had a profound impact on her. She also calls it a quiet, serene experience unmatched anywhere else on the globe. She witnessed an infinite number of fish dancing in a beautiful arrangement. Coral with candy-colored tones swayed beneath like a vibrant Monet. As colorful parrotfishes suddenly appeared and started eating algae from coral reefs, crabs were scrambling across the ocean floor.

You will experience nature's beauty when you are in it. You'll learn more about who you are. You will come to self-realization when you observe how individuals live in these circumstances. You'll learn just how hungry the underprivileged are! Being confined to the hut will cause you to achieve self-actualization and realize the worth of your life.

- **You become more responsible.**

You don't have these obligations when you travel with your family or friends. However, you must develop responsibility when you go alone. You must make your own decisions, and you are accountable for those decisions.

In Leh Ladakh, a region with a chilly peak covered in snow, Neha- one of my dearest friend- once went for a solo bike ride. She was in charge of her own security because she was by herself. Even though she had to go through the blazing sun during the day and the chilly breeze at night, she was content with the weather. She had the incredible experience of riding a bike alone, and she once described to me how she had gone for about 8 hours straight to get to Dharamshala. (Dharamsala is situated in the Himachal Pradesh district of Kangra.) There, she says, she was responsible for her own food and safety. Few people in the night, scared her a lot. The decision of staying close to the group of people ensured her safety on many occasions. Later in the day, she continued traveling. She talks about visiting a large waterfall and practicing meditation beneath it. She used to consume anything in her path, including snacks and meals at dhaba. The nicest solo excursion she had ever taken was this one. The best experiences in life will arrive when you are all by yourself, isolated.

You will learn your responsibilities and oversee your own safety. You must remain by yourself in a motel and find meals. This will assist you in becoming independent. You choose your own itinerary, including the places you go.

- **You get out of your comfort zone.**

Traveling to strange locations will push you to develop new skills and teach you to rely on yourself in stressful situations. You can assess your patience by stepping outside of your cozy home. I once attended a field trip for a warli painting and had a fantastic time from morning to evening. 20 km away from my place was nothing smaller. I had the opportunity to learn new things about adivasi culture and more. Diverse clothing and traditional ornaments amazed me. The individuals were dancing in accordance with their cultural traditions, and others were painting warli paintings on the walls. The whole village was decorated with warli paintings. The houses were made of grass and covered with cow dung. When you interact with a new tribe, you learn about their culture, traditions, diet, and attire.

After the field trip, we proceeded to a residence where they offered us bhakri and thecha, a traditional dish that is well-known in the southern region of India.

I was able to meet new people, get beyond my comfort zone, and communicate with them. It was a brief journey for me, but it taught me a lot about life and helped me become more outgoing.

You can only tour a beautiful planet and find a lot of fresh and amazing places if you put yourself there. In order to overcome these difficulties and develop into a new person, you will be tested to explain where you are going to a local, go trekking on a mountain, taste the local cuisine, etc.

The task for you: This weekend, go to a nearby mountain and explore new stuff.

- **You will learn how to rely on yourself.**

Traveling to different parts of the world will teach you how important it is to rely on yourself in trying circumstances. Make sure to trust your own feelings, your decisions, and your choices since you are the most important person in your life. That will assist you in making decisions and communicating them to others in the future. It will be beneficial for you to rely on yourself, understand that you are the creator of the world around you, and appreciate your own needs.

- **It will help to boost your confidence.**

You will learn many different abilities and develop more self-assurance if you go alone. Your ability to overcome problems will be improved by the experience of traveling alone, which will help you grow as a person and a good human being. A challenge in and of itself is traveling alone. And all the other things you have to handle and plan, showing that, with enough effort,***you can accomplish anything you set your mind to.***

Start investing before the age of 30

Yes, it is never too late to start! Money is the fuel for our evolving lives. When you start to invest the money before your 30s it can be more beneficial for you in your, let's say, 40s. As the Chinese proverb says "the best time to sow a seed was 20 years ago, the next best time is today." Ideally, the best time for investment is from the day you start to earn. You should inculcate the habit of investing money in yourself. **If you want to be and stay rich, most of your money should go into an asset and a little into a liability as per the need.**

-It will eventually help you to know the importance of money.

-By this age, you become more comprehensible about your goals. It will become easier to choose the right product for your investment.

-your income gets high, and you get to know how much money you get into your hands and how much for the bills.

-investing in a specific place or stock will gradually help you to increase your capital.

Consider "x" person has 5 crores in his/her hand and has 2 options in their favor.

1. To take a house or car and invest in it which will give u "zero" income or

2. To invest it in the bank or stock market which will give "lakhs" in income after a year.

So, it is necessary to have knowledge of how to save money and where to spend it.

-start investing for a long-term goal.

Remember, investing in a product like buying an automated machine for your industry is an easy thing. However, investing in stock and crypto needs concise knowledge. So, studying about the money multiplication is always the right thing to do.

Get known by at least 1000 people in a positive way

Isn't it incredible to be acknowledged by those in your immediate vicinity and having the title of "millionaire" before 30? with this thought and many dreams in his eyes, Mahesh moved to Mumbai. Beginning his modeling career in "the city of dreams" seemed thrilling. Mahesh gave his best at every opportunity he beholds but failed. On the bright side, it provoked him to follow his hobby- motivational speaking. Shiva once approached him. filled with despair after a string of failures his only hope lies in Mahesh. Mahesh explained to him a thing about life and gave him wonderful tips from the book- Unstoppable- that helped shiva in getting back to his work with a lot of energy and clarity to win over his life and achieve consecutive victories. This incident builds a surge of joy and faith within Mahesh. He developed his carrier into motivational speaking. Currently, with all his efforts and decisions paying off, he is a victorious entrepreneur as he started running his own company. Besides, Mahesh got incredibly famous for his inspirational free "Life-Changing Seminar". He is inspiring people across the world.

So, Mahesh is now unstoppable. When will you take your passion into public and get renowned? let us all become unstoppable and pursue our aspirations of creating our own dynasties and ruling over the world. When you gain a positive reputation, other people start to perceive and think similarly. **When your aura becomes stronger and you become influential, even the critics, unknowingly, follow you and you become unstoppable.**

Read 100 books before the age of 30

Do you know who can be your lifelong friend? A book. Reading for pleasure can progressively increase both your intelligence and your skill level. Your mental capacity will be improved. Many people find satisfaction in the activity of reading books. Unlike audio-visual videos, reading forces you to imagine the scene yourself thus increasing your imagination.

I, once, availed an opportunity to talk my old friend Tina during a book-writing webinar. I was surprised to know that Tina has already written five novels that were best sellers on amazon and is currently working on her sixth book. We took an informative walk during which she revealed the secret of her transformation from a distracted, hyperactive, ignorant girl to this. How reading became her best friend, and how she overcame her awful mental capabilities. I witnessed the moment when a teacher from our school advised her to do nothing but reading. "Just start reading. Even if you do not understand the meaning or context keep on reading and eventually you will start to understand" he said. He was right. Being a hyperactive girl and not good in studies, reading is the easiest act she could do. With a desperation to move out of the taunts from colleagues and insults from teacher and neighbors, Tina took the advices seriously and began reading. During the walk, she described how she used to finish 12 books in a year. Sometimes, entire book in a day used to be her threshold. Destiny separated us since then, but today I know what reading has done to her. She attributes books with greatly influencing who she is today. She gained a great deal of knowledge about becoming zero to a hero and how to feel satisfied with who you are. Her value increased exponentially and she lives among some of the most influential people. In present times, she is a well-known author and is successful.

It aids with personality development. They have been buddies forever. They aid in mental conditioning. They aid in stress relief for us. You will benefit much from reading works on biography, autobiography, fiction, and non-fiction. Educational textbooks and sci-fi books also are not a bad choice.

"Reading 100 books before 30" is a goal worth achieving since it inspires in us a wealth of life lessons and virtues that will serve us well in the years to come. Additionally, it promotes longer sleep cycles. Some of the books that helped me develop the best life lessons also helped me feel more confident and more like myself. The book "The magic of thinking big" by David Schwartz is the one I suggest most. **Reading a lot of books expands your mind and makes you capable of anything.**

"Sales, Negotiation, Human nature, and Money take these four subjects. Now, read any 25 books that are above four-star rating with 400 reviews on sales. Take Human nature, Psychology, and Persuasion; Read any book on any of those subjects. Then, read any book with above 400 reviews on Money. Now, for two years, obsess over doing that. Two years later, Work extremely hard, up to your 100 percent. Apply all that you have learnt and improve in marketplace, also figure out a way to improve your attitude." Remember, nobody likes the people who are constantly blaming somebody else. Now, after doing all these things, you will be winning the marketplace. You will be doing extremely well to live a life of wealth, satisfaction, happiness, and love. That is the power of knowledge, that is the power of effective reading.

Some of the books which are most recommended to read:

I. **Bhagavat Gita.**
II. **Atomic habits.**
III. **Ikigai.**
IV. **The subtle art of not giving a fuck.**
V. **How to win friends and influence people.**
VI. **The magic of thinking big.**
VII. **The magic of thinking what you want.**
VIII. **Think and grow rich.**
IX. **The power of the subconscious mind.**
X. **The psychology of money**

Learn one additional skill that can be developed as a carrier

"Once you stop learning, you start dying," which is just a satellite view of why learning is more essential in life. One of my close friends- Om- worked for a reputed computer company and had a respectable position. Despite an incredible professional life, loneliness and dissatisfaction daily awaited him at home. Sitting lonely in grief did not please him anymore. Though he found delight in his job, he, deep down, was attracted towards painting. When some individuals used to visit his place, they complimented him and advise him to take up painting as a full-time career. His talent as an artist is reflected through every painting at his house. Yet, a common belief in job security entangled him in a 9 to 5 rat race. The "Ding-ding" sound of his doorbell struck Om's ears once. "Hey, welcome", Om greeted Me. I saw the house shining with colors and designs on bright walls.

The paintings are grand, distinctive representations of events from everyday life. On canvas, some are designed. Some are created on fabric, while others are on gorgeous glasses and walls. I exclaimed, "All of these artworks greatly impressed me".

"Yes, I've loved painting since I was a little kid, and I love to put my creativity everywhere," Om proudly said. "Probably do not mind me saying but you are a great artist and I see your future very much successful in this profession rather than doing a 9 to 5 job," I said as I was perusing the area. I think the universe was on my side. After a month, he was fired due to the financial losses company faced and cannot afford the employee. But Om was not disturbed at all. He grabbed the opportunity and started selling paintings. Currently, he is making thousands of dollars monthly- more than he was making at his previous work.

You already possess a skill; recognize it and do it. You must have noticed that many individuals lost their jobs and were homeless during COVID-19. In life, we ought to always have a backup plan.

Future abilities are essential since they can boost your success and help you have better career chances as new professions are created by digital and artificial intelligence (AI) technology.

Even a skilled cook who starts their own vada-pav business might make more money than a corporate employee. What matters is how good your skill is. Once, my nearby aunt called while I was on my way home, and we had a pleasant conversation. I questioned her on "how she established her own business and developed herself". She described to me how she left her work after having her first child. and started her career in a modest shop after pursuing her passion for fashion design.

Developing new talent is essential for career advancement. It expands your pool of potential employers and aids in your development of fresh approaches to keep up with the world's rapid change.

Development of a skill, whose entire control is in your hands, makes you UNSTOPPABLE.

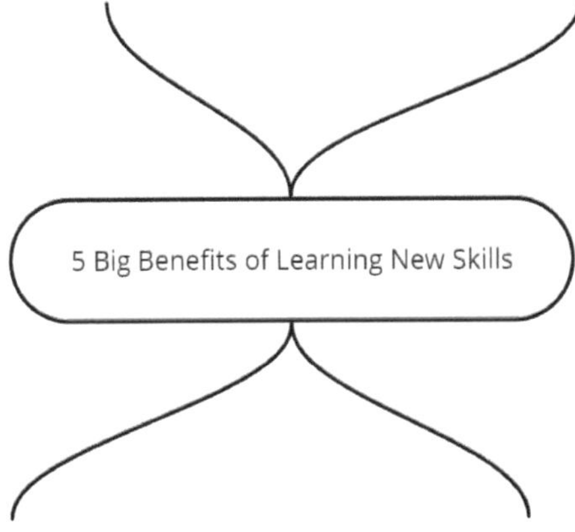

Fail miserably in something

"Those who dare to fail miserably can achieve greatly. But those who fail fast, achieve faster." You will never succeed unless you are prepared to fail. Failure is inevitable in a life compared to a roller coaster. But failing early in your life will give you success early. The best time to fail is when you have the most energy and emotional stability to handle the impact and try again. So, it is better that you try something new and fail before your 30s.

Have you ever reached your lowest point? You are aware of the phrase "there is only one way to go from rock bottom." It is a good idea but challenging to put into action when you are in the situation and up against insurmountable challenges that seem overwhelming.

I have fallen short practically everywhere in my life (okay, maybe some areas). I have made great mistakes at various points in time, sometimes all at once. As a child I must have failed at some point. I have tried dieting and failed. Additionally, I have failed in my studies too and. However, the truth is that I am not aware of a single successful individual who has never made a mistake. They are successful because they do not stay focused where they failed. They refuse to let failure define them.

Once I met Rhea, she is now a FOUNDER and CEO of a cosmetic company which worth 300 cr. Rhea is an alumnus of IIT Kanpur where she studied electrical engineering as well as IIM Ahmedabad, where she pursued her degree in business studies. It takes a lot for any one of us to even dream of a 1 crore job offer, let alone reject it. But Rhea had her mind and heart set on starting her venture since her MBA days. For her it was about making bigger changes and taking charge, being boss of her own life, and what better way than to start her own company. There was nothing that could have deflected her from her goals at that point, not even 1 crore. While the market was ready and the products were ready to go, Rhea had to overcome numerous obstacles to enter the digital-first beauty business. They were informed that solely selling online would make it tough to compete with other businesses. Her problems were not limited to that; as a woman in a male-dominated society, she had to deal with her fair share of casual sexism. Once, an investor refused to meet Rhea. He wanted to talk business with a 'man'. But she let her work do the talking. "Being a mother of 1, she also had to juggle motherhood with her work. At times she needs to be pumping breast milk, working out, handling office calls, & hoping to not wake her daughter up." After several sleepless nights of attempting to strike a balance between her personal and professional lives, it paid off for her. Her company was named one of the finest cosmetics brands in India! Failures happen, and life is NOT always sweet, but if you work hard enough and do not give up when you are down, you just might be able to find your path.

We learn via failure. This has been shown in the academic setting, the basic idea holds true in all facets of life. When everything is going well, there is little incentive to adjust or put effort into the areas that require it. Failure, though, has a way of drawing our attention.

- **Failure Leads to Innovation**

Scientist Alexander Fleming was attempting to create a new wonder medication, but it was not until he tossed away his unsuccessful tests and mold started to appear that he realized the mold was really eradicating the bacteria in the petri dish. Penicillin was created from mold in the trash. Amazing innovations that we now rely on were born out of total failure. You never know what incredible opportunity or invention might be created solely by an epic disaster. However, you must continue to study it and search for opportunities you had not before considered.

- **Failure Grows Resiliency**

When you fail you have two options – quit or find another way. With my first manuscript, I aimed to become a best-selling author. I preferred to follow the conventional route in order to work with a traditional publisher. But following the conventional course of action got me nowhere. I had to learn more when I failed. Expand more. Be better. Although I preferred the simple route, taking the difficult one made me stronger. I acquired expertise in a variety of fields, including writing, blogging, computer programming, web design, photography, social media, marketing, speaking, networking, etc. The finest part was that I gained writing skills. Failure is like hearing "that's not good enough" from your coach. And in that instant, each of us has the option to either give up or hear those comments and try to do it better. Many walls will halt you on your path to success. But it is only a dead-end if you turn around.

- **Failure Encourages Exploration**

Do you currently feel lost? Perfect! Just now, you completed the first phase of exploration. You are compelled to travel to the unknown countries nearby when your home is destroyed by fire. And with this imagine you had travelled many countries all over. Go Ahead, Fail

The biggest failure of our lives would be if we never had any.

Go ahead, fail. Fail big. Fail with gusto.

Just do not stop moving forward.

The path to success is paved with failure. Start pouring cement.

Thus, I conclude, achieving these milestones before your 30s will make your success easier. Make a note of every milestone, deduce a map of how to achieve it, and set a deadline to achieve it. This is your path to make your life easier; to make you UNSTOPPABLE.

III

13 Hacks To Save Money

Automate your savings

Be honest! When you get the money in your hand or bank account you endeavor to spend it. It is a common temptation in the materialistic world where money is meant to flow. Yet, we all relentlessly try to save money and multiply it to get a bigger materialistic gain. If you want to multiply your money, then you need to AUTOMATE YOUR SAVING.

Establishing regular transfers into your investment account is called Automating your savings. Making it automatic can help keep your savings plan on track no matter what else is going on in your life. Not only can you make saving automatic, but you may also be able to make investing automatic. Here is where you start building wealth without even giving time to it.

Learn how automating your investing can help make it easier to work toward your financial goal. You need to do SIP or make a new bank account. if you have a certain amount in your hand, then separate the amount for your daily use and deposit the desired amount in the investment account.

Recently, I had a call with my cousin. She just got married and started working towards building their dream life. Priya- with her husband Raj- used to live in a one-bedroom apartment with a large gallery. Both were employed in high positions by reputed companies. Each one of them made one lakh rupees a month. In India, this package seems to be high. They moved from a one-bedroom dwelling to a bungalow in a reputable neighborhood. Sometime later, buying their own dream car completed one more of their dream-life milestone. I wondered how they have been doing so well financially. My question was answered in the call with Priya. They used the tactics to save money, its automation, and money multiplication information as the key. After separating the GST and loans, they used whatever cash they had on hand. They used their respective bank accounts to pay their own expenses. And finally, they saved any remaining funds to multiply it. Once, Priya visited a shopping mall close to her home, she found a dress with an incredible diamond finish. It was priced at 3000 rupees, and she loved it. But all she could think about when making the purchase was, do I need it right away. Presumably, her instinct prevented her from buying. Therefore, it is important to consider where we should spend our money and how much we can save for the future. Money awareness is a beautiful and helpful part of the money-handling technique. Monetary awareness can save us from a lot of useless transactions. Money awareness played an important role in increasing the automation amount and achieving the couple's milestones faster.

If you are married, you must have 1 account for the husband and another for the wife. The third will be a joint account for savings. You will make personal transactions from your respective bank accounts. So, in the end, a high amount will be saved in the third bank account. You should know where you must spend the money and on what material.

Now, why do you need to save? **To invest and reinvest**.

With-hold from spending money

Do you perform the fasting ritual?

Here is the point, let us do fasting for 1 day in the entire month, week, or in 15 days. A non-spending day where you will not spend any money the entire day even if you need anything. How does it work? You will definitely get more disciplined. Like if you do not have permission to spend the money you will preplan all kinds of stuff and you will not spend any money on useless stuff. Try not to spend any amount of money one day a month. If you want to spend the "x" amount on anything, just stop and prevent the transaction. This is your non-transaction day.

When returning from exercise, there used to be food stalls on the side of the road selling items like samosas, sandwiches, kachoris, and other fast food. Even though it was my non-spending money day, my heart encouraged me to eat something. Heart questioned, "How much money will be spent for just 40 rupees." However, I stood firm in my choice to follow this no-spend day. I returned home with a heavy heart and made a healthy meal, an "Upma." I was able to save 40 rupees that day with the help of this, and those 40 rupees were added to my savings accounts.

With this habit, you will be saving a lot of money. **The habit of saving money is an education.** It cherishes every asset. Teaches self-denial and cultivates a sense of order. Trains to the foresight and so broadens the mind. Art is not making money but sustaining it. The more you will be saving and investing the more it will be beneficial for you in your future life.

As well said by Warren Buffett ***"Do not save what is left after spending but spend what is left after saving."***

This will help you to understand:

- The importance of disciple and saving money.
- Money cannot buy everything.

- You will have to plan your day without money this will teach you to value your money.
- Will learn to save and invest more.

Use UPI instead of credit cards

The money that you use from UPI belongs to you it is your own money but the money you use from credit cards is from the bank. Credit card money is a debt to us, it is not ours. It needs to be paid. Moreover, whenever you pay cash from a credit card surcharge of 1%, 2%, or 3% is, sometimes, applied. Thus, surely, that is not the smart way to do it. Why do u want to pay that, when UPI is absolutely free? Let us make ourselves smarter rather than just the mobile. UPI is YOUR money; it withdraws from your bank account. And if you do not have money then do not spend it. Why live a life in debt? That helps to be disciplined about money. Better than mindlessly spending a huge sum using a credit card, right?

UPI	credit card
MONEY BELONGS TO YOU	MONEY IS DEBT ON YOU
ITS FREE	SURCHARGE IS APPLIED
MONEY IS IN BANK	MONEY LOANED TO YOU

USE CREDIT CARDS ONLY WHEN YOU HAVE 100% MONEY

3 Benefits of using a credit card: -

- Using a credit card is not a bad idea or you may use it when you have 100% money to pay back. You are spending money for a whole month and paying it after 30 to 45 days; this means somebody is legitimately giving you a month interest-free loan.

- If your credit card spending is too high by putting the same amount in a debit mutual fund at least you will earn a little interest. Yes, it will not be much but it is free money then why not?

- Whenever you use a credit card your credit rating improves according to your payments so you will always make a full payment every month and that will boost your credit score.
- While Using credit cards you are offered lots of rewards and vouchers. With this, you can save money and invest it.

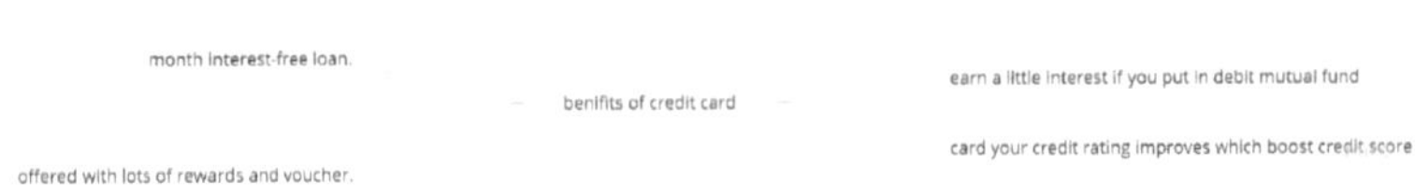

Make your shopping list

I went shopping once, with my parents. It was just a matter of a few T-shirts for me. I went to D-Mart, got in, took the trolly, scanned the place, and went to the clothing section. We found the desired T-shirts, I tried them on, and we were done. Right? Wrong. Like everyone else there, my parents went through the rabbit-hole too.

They started moving around, looking around. I told them that the goal is accomplished, and there is nothing more to buy. “Let’s see what we need at home” mom replied. Searching without knowing what to search for is similar to scrolling YouTube without knowing what to watch. Both waste your time, energy, and MONEY because of my parents. Like all else end up buying a lot of additional products. Does this happen to you? Be honest! The shopping list is the most important tool that defines the quality and accuracy of your shopping. This will gradually help you to get into discipline. Not only the discipline in shopping but the acquisition of focus and clarity in other tasks as well. You need to prioritize the things which you want or basically, you will end up buying things that you never wanted and wasting a lot of money. When we do not have a shopping list, we often end up buying food items that we already have at home. Because food is perishable, buying more than you can consume is a bad, awfully bad idea. It ultimately develops into habits and leaves you broken.

Tina, my best friend, was getting married, so she wanted to go shopping before attending the ceremony at her home. When her wedding finally arrived after 10 days, I was without the items she needed to bring for the wedding ceremony. Nearly saving time and money, I completed my shopping in a more efficient manner. The question is "how?" I created a lengthy shopping list before going shopping and jotted down the items that were required. This includes a dress, bracelets, a gift for her buddy, etc. I completed all the necessary shopping when I went to the mall. A large watch boutique with watch models shown on a large screen caught Tina’s attention as she was walking past it in a hallway and drew her inside. She noticed numerous smartwatches with square, round, and various themes that were all reasonably priced and of high quality. But she reasoned that she already owned a watch that was in fine shape and had just recently been purchased, so she was not in immediate need of another. And a watch was not on her list of things to buy. She eventually left the store without making an “additional” transaction. Through this occurrence, she was able to avoid wasting money on items she does not necessarily need.

Shopping lists tend to reduce transactions because it reminds the shopper of his/her goals and makes planned/needed purchases more obvious. It also helps us with making a list of all the items that we need on an urgent basis so that we do not forget them.

Once you figure out what you want and what material or food item you want and how much cash you are going to spend then carry only that amount into the store. Then, there is no way you can overspend.

Also, online whenever you are buying make a shopping list and stick to what you want! And whatever is required buy that and move out. Do not misuse your money.

Enter Caption

The 30-day rule

I once went to a finance seminar held by a well-known professional with an intense knowledge of finance and business management. He shared an ocean of knowledge, except for one that caught my special attention. The "30-Day Rule" helped me manage my finances and save and multiply money. Once I came across a great showpiece to display over my beautiful bookshelf on the wall. I read the reviews and was about to make a transaction on amazon when the 30-day rule hit my memory. I was following it. I stopped and decided to buy it after 30 days. Why? Allow me to explain.

This rule is a brilliant psychological hack. Following this, whenever you want to buy something big or something which you want now but is of no use later then just stay back and ask yourself after 30 days. Do I need that showpiece? Was it important to me at that time? The answer will be 'NO'. This is how you will be able to resist too. Whenever there will be a sale, or an offer buy the things which are necessary for you instead of buying the unnecessary ones.

The 30-day rule is a simple strategy that has the power to help you control your spending and otherwise make the right financial choices for you. Why there is a 30-day rule? With the 30-day savings rule, you delay all non-essential purchases for 30 days. Instead of spending your money on the spot you are availing 30 days to think about it. At the end of these 30 days, if you still want to make that purchase, go ahead. Else, you may drop the transaction plan.

This rule will change your attitude toward spending and saving and help you to maintain your budget. **The 30-day rule will also help you with a lifestyle change and will help you to navigate your approach toward financial discipline.** And sometimes you might forget to buy that product, or it goes out of stock. This will help you to increase your patience level and will make you aware of your needs.

Lease items for occasional use

If you are using anything occasionally then take it on rent. Nowadays, you get everything on rent like a dress, car, and gadgets. If you do not use it often, then please take it on rent.

you have a career in modeling and for every function or program, you do not need to buy a new dress worth lakh. You can just rent it.

If you have a passion for photography and you want to click some photos of wild animals or anything you just can take the camera on rent. Instead of buying if you are doing it rarely.

I once read in an interview about Sonam Kapoor (she is a celebrity and model) that she rents her clothes most of the time because she only wears them once, which helps her save money and avoid wasting it, rather than purchasing pricey lehengas worth 10 to 15 lakhs. Even most females in Navratri rent “ghagra” dresses rather than purchasing them.

Tanu, one of my friends, told me of a situation in which she had to rent her Mumbai home rather than buy it because of a transfer and the need to move; rather than spending a large sum of money on a home, it was better to stay on rent.

When you rent the things automatically you may save money from buying just renting them instead of buying and it will keep you away from buying things that you use rarely. Renting new clothes will add a new collection to your fashion.

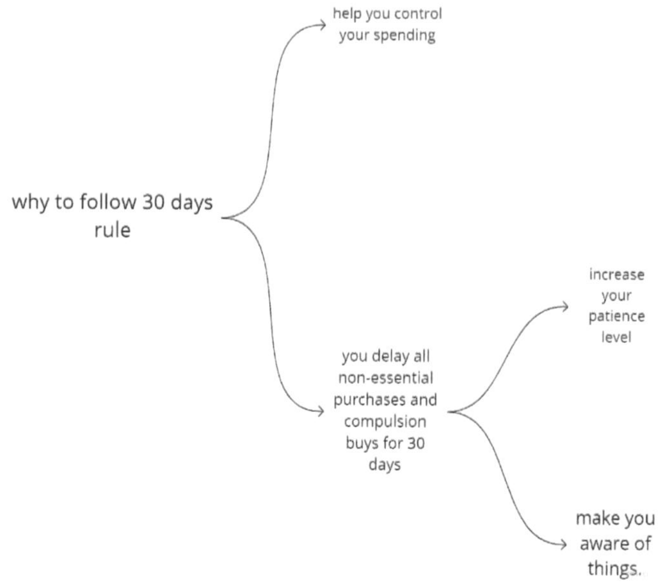

Buy big sizes of consumables

I think the topic of the shopping list and this goes hand in hand. A shopping list though seems to be conveying the suggestion that buys according to your "needs" but it certainly does not mean that as a whole. You see, the world kept suggesting to us that we must shop as per our needs. If you need one chocolate to buy one chocolate. If you need the book "A brief history of time" buy only that book. Do not spend your money on unwanted things like buying one more chocolate or one more book with it. However, I doubt that. And the further explanation will make it clear that by using this incredibly old teaching you are emptying your pockets for less.

Last month, I ordered two books on amazon to read. My only need and want was "Psychology of Money." Now, I want you to go on amazon and check the price of the book- Psychology of money and the subtle art of not giving a fuck. At the time I am writing this chapter, both the prices add up to Rs. 453. Now, this would be the price I needed to spend if I would have taken both books one by one as per the need. However, the author is clever. I bought both books at once and that cost me Rs. 229. I saved Rs. 224. I bought both books paying less than the price of one book. Now, this is called smart shopping. So, make a shopping list, but use it wisely to save your money. Add these two learnings to your smart shopping skill.

The point is- "Purchase a large number of items for future use due to the high expense per unit of small sizes." Therefore, the difference between a Maggi big and small is clear. If you purchase a small tea, it will cost more than a large tea. Thinking about the future use of purchased items should be considered. These futuristic-but-smart transactions need precautions such as checking the expiry date of desired goods. You will save per unit as a result, which is a wise method to save costs. When we purchase fewer units, we end up spending more because the per-unit cost is higher. This is how you do smart shopping.

Shop online in incognito mode

Have you ever wondered how does your computer know you want to buy a laptop or a car? How does YouTube know you are searching for an IIT-prep class? The computer knows it because you search for it on it. The websites where you look for certain items store something called cookies. These cookies contain your search activity information. This allows the website to capture your search and recommend related products at the right prices and offers. They show you a discounted model of the laptop that you search for the most and create urgency by showing you that the offer ends soon. Now, the same tricks are played by YouTube and other social media platforms that cost your time for their products. But when you enter the shopping world Amazon plays a leading role.

Such shopping platforms play with a price. In most cases, the prices and offers are personalized so you buy the product as soon as possible while making a desirable profit for the company. All this is done by cookies. Moreover, cookies also store your private information like credit card information and your email passwords. The data can be shared to earn a huge profit for the company. Due to strict laws, these selling activities have considerably reduced but your data is with multiple companies besides yours. How to save your privacy and shop for the products without getting manipulated by the market? Here, we will specifically talk about shopping anonymously. The secret is- "not giving away information through cookies." How? By using chrome's incognito mode.

If you search for the same thing frequently the rate of that thing starts to increase. This creates an urgency in you, and you buy the product before the price increases more. But Incognito allows the user to stay anonymous and the activities do not stay anywhere on the computer. So even if you search for a laptop 100 times, on amazon, it will always be your first time. And this saves you from manipulation and gets the item for you at a reasonable and real cost. So anytime you want to buy online try to buy it in incognito mode so that the website will not be able to access your information and they will give you the best price that is provided to a new user which more often is the lowest price. Lowest because they want the new user to convert into a loyal customer buy from their website or app. Anonymity is not possible in apps, instead use laptops or desktops and save money.

Buy life insurance early in life

Readers, understand that '**your money has limited time to grow.**' It is foolish to believe that your money can grow anytime in life and at the same speed. If you invest money in the market or policies or banks doing FDs and RDs, it is universally true that time matters more than the growth of the market or the value of the currency. In your 20s, your health is good. The probability of your hospitalization is exceptionally low. Your death probability is exceptionally low. Besides even the best time to try various businesses is this time as your parents are looking after you may save money and invest it in these things. **Talking about insurance, the 20s is the best time to get life insurance at a very cheaper price for the same coverage due to health advantages.** Your money will have more time to grow if you purchase life insurance when you are young. Investing this early also increases the death or maturity benefits you will receive at the end of the policy's term. As you get older, your premium starts to increase for the same cover. Then, why not buy it at an early age? Early life's high income makes paying for insurance easy.

During the Covid-19 era, when everyone was locked down in homes a tragedy occurred. John had a migraine, and it got worse as COVID-19's second month progressed. With his bursting head, he barged out of the house to search for medical care. The medical facilities were all closed, and the migraine was taking over quickly. The health stole his sleep. It seemed like someone was banging a hanger on his head. He then contacted a reputed doctor in Mumbai, who advised doing an emergency procedure. Which was 10 lakhs in price. And managing money for him was extremely difficult. Upon inquiry, He received the money from the company as a result of a life insurance policy. He was, fortunately, able to conduct the treatment and get his good health back.

Your loved ones may benefit from having access to money when they need it. You may prepare for your family's long-term financial needs by understanding life insurance. Moreover, it makes your emergency an easy situation to pass. It works as a good fortune in times of health needs.

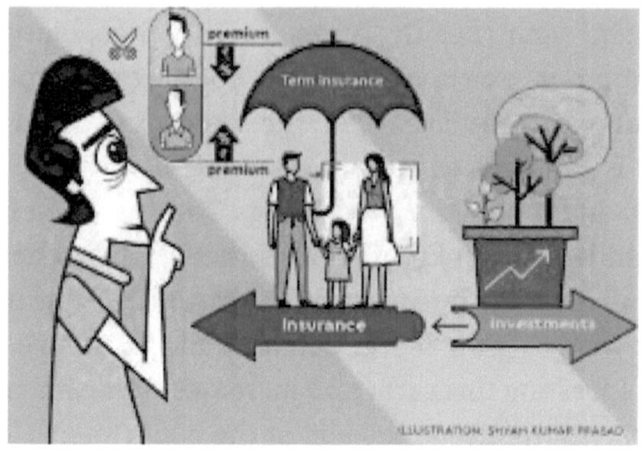

Develop a financial budget

Budget, budget, budget!!! "I have this budget; I have that budget; I want this thing, but it is not under my budget; Hurray! this year my budget increased" and so on. Why does everyone talk about the budget so much? Have you ever wondered about the importance of a budget? I have! Did you notice what leads to your decision to buy anything in life? I did! And yes, it is "budget." Budgeting is essential in our lives. In a world where riches are seen in net worth, the budget stays unnoticed. However, upon observation, we notice that rich also means someone with a high budget. We must learn to treat money as fuel. People tend to spend the fuel of life unnecessarily, which eventually ends their ride in the worst conditions. But budgeting stops your fuel from wasting. Budgeting is not a normal act of thinking; it needs sheer math, calculation, and prediction. It is the track record of the money that you spend. Nature of money proves- "Budgeting can feed without ever having to be called poor." Here is how budgeting works!

Rahul and Priya are a couple studying and planning to live in Pune. So, after a simple get-together, we were discussing how they are managing and spending their money. "Budgeting is essential, and we adhere to the 50-30-20 formula", Rohan professionally acknowledged. I expressed my curiosity to know more. "Our 50% of the revenue that we earn from the job is spent on food. Sometimes we make our own and sometimes we order it. Rest goes in clothing and educational materials," Priya explained. "And the remaining 30% is allocated to Sunday hikes or socializing with friends" Rahul continued. Where is the saving? The remaining 20% is saved in their bank accounts, which we will use when needed. This was the 50-30-20 rule that intrigued me and impelled me to research more on it.

The '50-30-20 rule" is the simplest to understand, easy to follow, and the most efficient budgeting technique, **unless you run a corporate**. This basically means 50 % of your income is spent on your needs like EMI, food, clothing, education, and bills; 30% of your income will be spent on your wishes like going on vacation and buying a mobile; the remaining 20 % will be a strict investment into your future like the investment, FD, or self-development course that will multiply your money. This habit guarantees financial abundance, awareness, and discipline in your life.

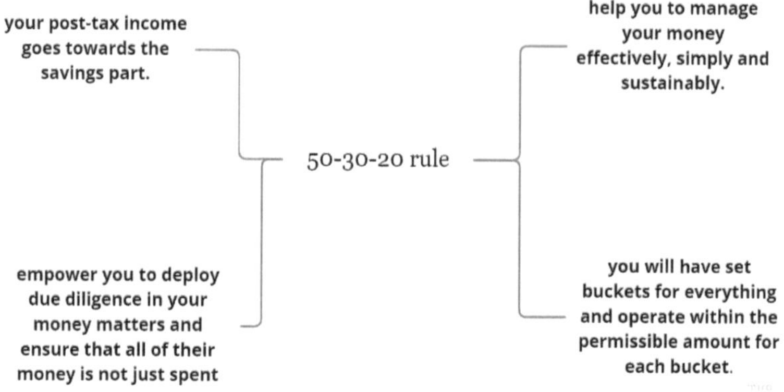

Use deals and discounts

As much as it seems obvious, it is important too. Use deals and discount sites as much as you can. Nearly every customer seeks discounts to save money while purchasing. Using coupons and discounts helps you to buy desired products while saving money. You may create your own discounts on shopping by breaking the marketing matrix. Use different tools and tricks, "Buy big sizes of consumables" being one of the tricks. Such discount creating and using shopping is what I call hacked shopping I have many personalized experiences with hacked shopping. I still remember one of them. A few weeks back, I was planning a rocket model for my rocket startup- AstroLab- and I needed a few supplies. There is no good stationery store near my place, so I searched on amazon. I noted the discounts there. Then, I went on google, of course in incognito mode, and search for the same product. There were so many sites and different discounts. Products were a pen knife, some wooden boards, and a pack of balloons. After searching well enough, I got all three products at huge savings. I saved almost Rs. 300. The other week I needed a few supplies again and upon not finding any at a good price I went out and found a good shop. Now, here I made a deal; "I will buy goods from you every time and make you a permanent supplier for my startup, but you have to give me the products at a wholesale cost" I proposed. And yeah! I got the deal and bought those products for a price cheaper than those on all the other sites I saw. Moreover, I got a supplier as well, so no worries about getting the desired product next time.

Next, you should consider buying fewer items while using coupons and discounts which will help to maximize your savings. Also, if you follow the 30-day rule, you will have a chance to avail greater discount on the desired product. In 11th standard, I needed a mobile phone as the lockdown made me study online. My parents chose 'The Redmi Note 9 Pro' for me and bought it for around Rs. 17,000. And now, a few days back, I checked its price as my father wanted to get a new mobile. I was surprised to see its price went down to 10,000. But the next time it will no more be surprising. The biggest benefit of the application of this entire topic is that you save money, and that money you may invest into other stuff which means it helps for multiple purchases.

Saving a small amount soon builds up a large amount.

Do not focus a lot on saving money; build money and enjoy it to the fullest

There is always going to be some amount of money that you need to spend, but saving is not always a solution. You do not have to give up on your luxury. This means you can always cut expenses but there is one thing you can increase as much as you can and that is your "Income." **The majority of your Focus should be on growing income then it can go far faster than you can save money**. Saving money will generate 1 crore in 20 years while generating money will make it in just 2 years or shorter. Moreover, you get more mature and improve over time in the quest of developing your income stream. And, with the job, you can make multiple side income streams. The best solution for this would be. "Those who don't manage or multiply money will always work for those who do."

IV

Selfish Tips For Better Life

Happiness is your number 1 priority

Until you are not happy, people around you will never be happy for you. If you do not find where your happiness lies so eventually you need to find the roots of what is making you unhappy.

On the second point- Once you got that make it a priority. If you want anything to happen in your life you need to design, it. Painting, for instance, if you like it do it. Make out time for it. How? Use a focus list. It is a new method that increases your focus and allows you to take up fewer tasks in a day while still completing your major goals. Putting your happiness first place is also good for your mental health. Being aware of what is not good for you and making the decision to make yourself happy can positively affect your mental health. But there is a difference. Majority of people take comfort zone and pleasure as happiness. But the happiness is to set free from that comfortable but unhealthy zone and conquer the short pleasure to live for greater success by delayed gratification.

Once, as I was driving along a road in the evening and admiring the setting sun with an orange sky, I noticed an elderly woman trying to cross the street. Swinging a bag in one hand and a wooden stick in the other, she looked vulnerable in her white hair and a white saree with a slight curve in her back. Due to traffic on the road and the time of day, cars were constantly passing one after the other. I went to her after spotting her and asked, "Would you like to cross the street"? The elderly woman responded to my question, "Yes child, I want to go to a shop across the street. "I then drop her off at the store while supporting her fragile hands. "God bless you, child," she blessed ending our meeting.

This small interaction filled me with happiness. Why? It is quite an obvious thing to feel the same for others being social animals. If you saw a happy man, you get happy, but a sad person's view drains your energy and turns your mood down. The golden rule of happiness is the more you make others happy the happier you will be. When you see yourself happy then the environment around you too will seem to be ecstatic. I am not saying to help someone but observe the depth of the act. We get happy after helping someone because we are meant to do that. We are social animals. This shows that you feel happy when you do something you are meant to do. Painting, singing, and music, are all skills that come to you naturally. Even solving physics can come naturally to you and you get happiness out of doing it. The first step in seeking happiness is to seek the cause of your unhappiness. In the world of the profession, most probably your happiness is due to the feeling of getting stuck with work that is not meant for you. Now, there are certain skills to develop an interest in what you do. But we will go into it in our webinars and seminars. Long story short, happiness lies in the things that are meant to be done by you. Therefore, it is the truth that another person will not be happy with the thing that makes you happy.

The acts that you are meant to do can be defined by knowing your vision and mission. Vision is the way you want the world to be, and mission is the long-term activity that you will do to make the world the way you want it to be. Today, the world is hopping upon the third stone of goals and ends up selecting uncertain goals. Thus, they fail to achieve their goals and end up working on someone else's goals. The mismatch in these goals creates a series of tasks and rituals that brings unhappiness. So, to find ultimate happiness know your vision and mission, then set your goals and deadline around that mission. Then move up and create monthly, weekly, and daily tasks. And just focus on these tasks and complete them using the focus list method. Now, on the final stone, make your daily rituals that are food for your mind and soul. One type of recommended ritual is a GIVER ritual.

- Gratitude is what we call living in the present. Thank the universe for all that you have after waking up with complete emotion. Now, enjoy the vibes you will get in.
- Imagination is the base of visualization. Imagine yourself in the position of achieving the goals you want and completing your mission to live your vision.
- Visualization is the quickest way to attract your goal. Imagination is in the mind while visualization spreads out to your entire body. When you feel the thing that you imagine via the five senses, then it becomes visualization.
- Exercise and eat right to take your body and mind to the highest potential. It is scientifically proven that mental development through physical exercise is far better than done via various brain games.
- Reading, leaders are readers. Reading "non-fiction" every day and completing at least one book a month will change your perspective to see the world. This ritual is a game changer and can be experienced fully only when done.

I challenge you to follow this ritual for one month with other self-development techniques and you will witness an incredible level of productivity and potential in yourself.

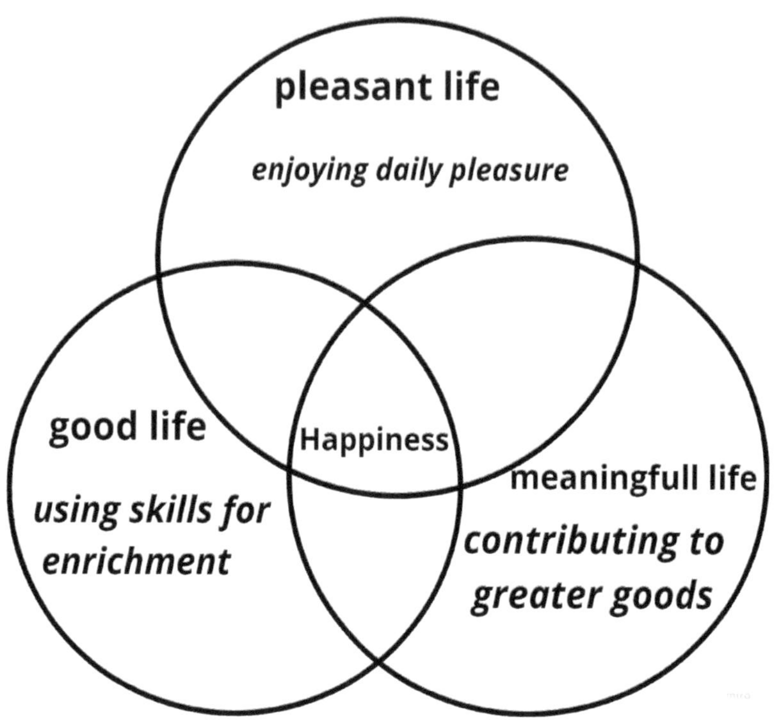

Do not give anyone the right to make you unhappy. You should be responsible for your own happiness as the input depends on others, but the response depends on you. When you are happy everything will fall into place because happiness takes you at a high vibration and the Law of Attraction works exactly right on that vibration. The secret to the magical powers of saddhus is the same. They live in a blissful state (High vibrations) all the time, thus the thing that they wish for happens out of the thin air.

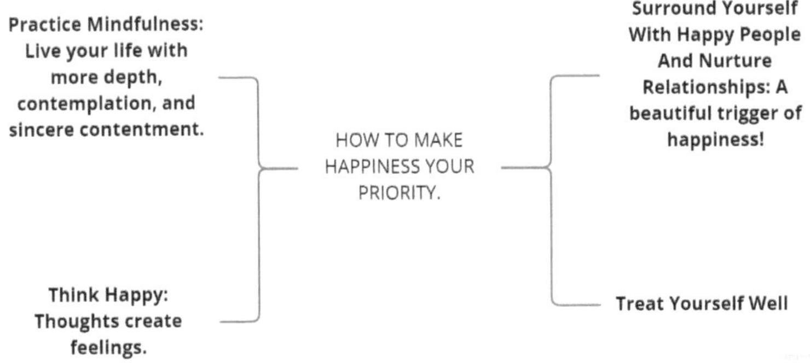

Enter Caption

Eliminate negative people from your life

I will share with you the tale of Jane, who was a teenage girl surrounded by worthless people who were there to spend their day's bunking classes, roaming here and there, with a lost vision on no mission.

One night, she was browsing her social media and came across the profile of her old friend- John. This completely transformed her life. Being childhood friends, they were already familiar with each other. They began to communicate online, and as time went on, their friendship grew. John took note of Jane's lifestyle, her friends, and her associates. He spoke about the value of surrounding oneself with productive people and impressed Jane with his philosophies for life. It moved Jane to the deepest of her personality.

Jane eliminated negative individuals, bringing her down. The change came to her in the form of peace, self-awareness, lightness, and a burning desire to succeed. As this occurred, she began to grow. She recognizes her worth. Her development as a person pleased her parents. She began to adore herself and started to build her empire with John. **The ability to surround yourself with positive people**

and maintain a positive attitude has a great impact on your life.

People began to feel appreciation for her. She began to receive praise from others.

John was the ideal person for her and significantly improved her quality of life. It is stated that when you have the proper person by your side, you can conquer the entire world. People are your habits, if not choose wisely they will ruin everything for you.

The less you will respond to negative people the easier your life will become. You need to associate with the people that inspire you. People that challenge you to rise higher. People that make you better. It is good to stay with people who are condemning you but have the intention to push you ahead by building rage into you. There are two ways of getting rid of negative people. First, be with positive people and negative people will disappear automatically. Second, ignore negative people completely and do not even think about them, thus stopping them from coming into your mind in the first place. This ultimately stops them from coming into your life too. The moment you do so you will start feeling positive and this positive feeling is important to you more than anything in the world!

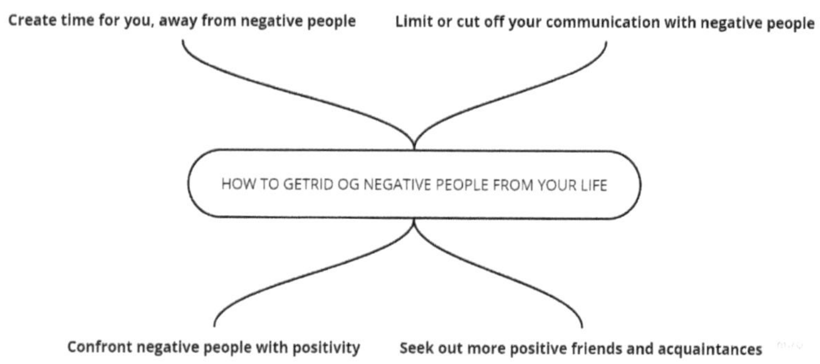

Cool rules for life

- The 2 min rule

An activity should be carried out immediately if it will take less than two minutes to complete.

If you get any task that is possible to be completed in 2 min or less, then do it there and then. Do not just keep it for later. Saying that this will be done. It is better to complete the task as soon as possible instead of postponing it. This will help to banish procrastination and will help you to complete a small task. If you can do an action in two minutes or less, tackle it at the moment — and do not delay.

For instance, it is incredibly difficult to complete a marathon. A 5K is difficult to run. It is challenging to walk 10,000 steps. Walking for 10 minutes is simple. Additionally, putting on your running shoes is simple. Putting on your running shoes may be your gateway behavior even though your ultimate objective is to run a marathon.

Before a lengthy yoga class, setting out your yoga mat and making space for it are examples of applying the concept to larger chores. You can also open your notes and arrange them before studying and decide that arranging notes makes it compulsory to study. Now, arrange it and study!!!

The two-minute rule helps you maintain the identity you want. You can vote for your new identity by attending the same location five days in a row, even if only for two minutes. You do not stress about staying in shape. Your goal is to develop into someone who consistently attends workouts. The smallest action you are taking is confirming the kind of person you want to be.

We rarely consider a change in this manner because everyone is preoccupied with the result. However, performing one pushup is preferable to doing nothing. Less is better than more when it comes to practicing the guitar. Reading for even one minute a day is preferable to never picking up a book. Better to accomplish less than you had intended than to take no action at all.

If you want to stop procrastinating and reach your goal faster, then try the 2 min rule. It should take less than 2 min to do 'James

Clear', the author of "atomic habits" says, it is better to take a book and read for 1 min rather than never pick it up. It is far better to do less than you hoped for than to do nothing.

How may you start 2 min rule?

You eventually start to reap the benefits of the trees you planted but initiating the process and having faith in it is essential. You will not succeed in your goals if you start an exercise routine just for the sake of starting one. Enjoy the exercise, have faith in yourself, and concentrate on the procedure. Results invariably start to flow in once it gets established.

The 2-minute rule should be kept in mind when deciding whether to participate in that delicious slice of cake in front of you as a cheat meal. Before you leave, turn around your head. **The little steps are what count**. Undoubtedly, small drips add up to an ocean.

- Fundamental relationship rule

Change the relationship, not yourself if you must change to become someone you dislike in a relationship. Moving to go from those that bring you down and give you bad vibes is preferable. Living by your own rules is preferable. In a relationship when you are not appreciated and valued, the first.

You surely need to do is just get out of it. Never love anyone who treats you like an ordinary. The Perfect Relationship is where you start to grow together rather than letting your graph down. "**Never lose yourself in a relationship.** Love your partner fiercely, but always follow your unique dreams and desires. Be true to yourself." You do not need to change yourself for a toxic person. If you will stay in a toxic environment, then your life too will become hell. So, it is better to remain alone rather than live in that relationship. "Stop setting yourself on fire to keep someone else warm"

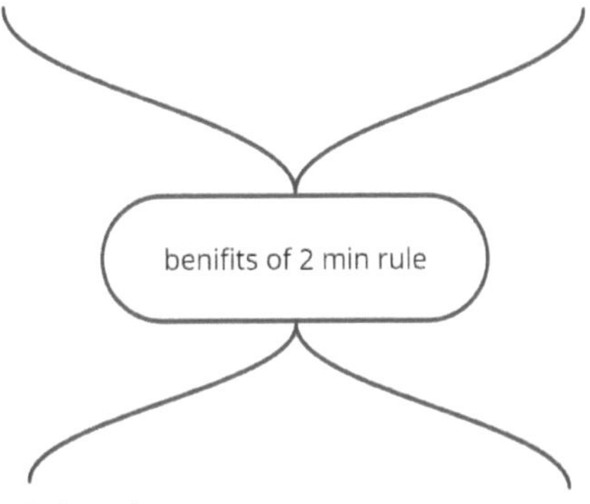

3 Things true friends do

- **They are genuinely happy about your success.**

- A true friend is one who is genuinely happy about your success.
- They help you to grow.
- They are always with you in your happy and sad times.
- Does not judge you
- Does not put you down or deliberately hurt your feelings.
- They are kind and respectful to you.
- someone whose company you enjoy.

- They are loyal to you.
- laughs with you.

- **Trustworthy and willing to tell you the truth, even when it is hard for you to hear.**

"Tell a lie once and all your trust becomes questionable"

The best friend is the one who never hides anything from you despite knowing that it will hurt you. **Telling the bitter truth is better than hiding it under a sweet lie**. It takes 1000 years to build trust, but to break it only takes a few sec.

The truth may hurt for a little while but a lie hurt forever. A true friend will never try to hurt you. The only quest he/she is on is to improve and grow you. He/ she will never make you sad by hiding anything from you. Knowing that truth will be hard, and you might not talk to them after that. Yet they state it because it is the right thing to do. In life have a friend like a mirror and a shadow. The mirror never lies the and the shadow never leaves!

3 Mistakes to not make in a relationship

- **Do not please everyone**

Often, we do things that are driven by one thought- "is the person pleased?." This thought process is the root of a few considerable psychological and physiological problems. FOMO, fear of missing out is one of them, Anxiety is another, Split personality disorder comes under this as well. Well, all these are at a high level of the people-pleasing job.

"You can't satisfy/please everyone" is a simple but compelling statement.

So usually, you do what others like but the more you will give control of your happiness to others the more unhappy you will become. Acceptance of this phrase is a mere step towards staying happy and self-satisfied. Low confidence, low self-esteem, and excessive shame are all problems of shifting focus from within to without.

Trying to please everyone is a recipe for stress and frustration. “You are the best as you are! You have this life to express yourself not to impress.” This is a common statement your friends and a lot of people say to you. Whoever, there is a deep meaning within. Before acting on this statement, you surely need to analyze yourself. Sometimes, we become destructible to society and loved ones. With this behavior, it is foolish to apply this statement. Rather than pleasing everyone or anyone, you must analyze yourself and see if there are wounds of guilt, fear, anger, and all other low-frequency abstract gadgets. And there should be some. Then, repair yourself along with dealing with people by asking two questions- “is the act I am doing positive for me?” and “is the act I am doing positive for the desired person and my environment?” If the answers are yes, go ahead and do it.

The mandatory thing is self-analysis. No-people-pleaser Does not allow you to harm people and act the way your ‘senses’ tell you. It is the phrase guiding you towards inner inspiration and analysis.

Everyone around you who listens to you has a different perspective and you cannot please everyone. Try to understand yourself, your thoughts, and your emotion. The best thing is to debate between your and the second person’s perspective. The winner’s perspective is the best! Do not lower your standards to fit in, rather try to take your environment up! Do not shrink who you are to make others comfortable. A growth mentality is a rare mentality. Yet, it has the utmost power. You must use it to upgrade your environment. But, if you see yourself getting blunt, it should be hard for you to leave the place immediately. This is called the application of detachment. This condition arises in relationships as well. If you see yourself or your partner getting blunt in a relationship and were sharp before, then you both should try to understand the wrong stuff and make it the right stuff.

After self-analysis and improvement, the word- "pleasing" does not matter anymore. You become a natural magnet. Yet, it is not all good, and here is where you should use- "I am the best as I am." Non-people-pleaser does not always mean you cannot please everyone. The game of focus and awareness, and effort sometimes makes you a natural magnet. Dr. APJ Abdul Kalam is a great example of that. He almost had no haters. He did not please people. He upgraded and inspired people in a pleasing way. Questioning, meditation, and awareness are the best ways of self-analysis. The book will talk more about it ahead.

- **Do not judge people!**

Do not judge anyone until you get to know them. You must have heard the beautiful phrase "never judge a book by its cover" this basically means what you see from the outside is not what really is. When we are small, we often think that people who drink, smoke, or do parties are not nice people. But what you do is not your personality what you are inside, what you think, and the worldview that you have that establishes your personality and your nature.

The more you judge others the more you judge yourself. By constantly seeing bad in others our brain gets trained to find bad this can lead to an increase in stress and anxiety. Each person is different from others. Remember people have 1 thing in common that is all are different. If you do not like something that does not mean that the other person too should not like it. For e.g.: if the other person is going shopping on weekends you just can't say shopping is boring. People can do what they want! That is why to stop judging people from your own preference. When people know you are judgmental, they often take a step back and think 2 times before saying anything.

When you point your finger at others but you are pointing at yourself too. People like to stay around positive people. positive people put out positive energy and fun around. But when you are with a negative person the vibes which you sense are negative. The more you attract good things the more life will be good. So, decide what you want to be? a judging person or a positive person?

- **Do not always solve problems**

If someone comes to you with a problem, it's not necessary that you should always solve it. Often males do it, young boys. We think that we must solve the problem but most people who have come to you want that you should hear the issue. Anyone should just listen to them without judging, ignorance but not to solve the problem. And if you can be that person then that is the best gift you can give them at that moment.

When someone comes to us in a state of overwhelm, the greatest gift we can give Them is to listen with our full attention, make eye contact, allowing all emotions to be present in them.

When we refrain from trying to fix their problems, we empower them to fix them for themselves. We have an opportunity to lighten someone's load just by allowing them to set it down in front of us and have us acknowledge it. We do not have to solve it for them. Relationships are made stronger when we can be present in the way others need us to be. Learning to show up for people not only enhances their lives but our own.

Enter Caption

Things you should not apologize for

- **The clothes you wear.**

The clothes you wear define your personality. So, the way you show the people see from that point of view. You will just apologize to everyone, and think will they like it or not then you will never know yourself better. Never feel ashamed for the way you look or the way you dress or the way you feel and do not ever apologize for that thing. You are who you are, and you are beautiful in your own way. A person is known by his behavior and his personality and not by which type of clothes has been wore. You do not have to wear expensive clothes to look good. It is not about the clothes you wear but the life you lead in the dress. However, there is always psychological criterion we abide by. So, make sure to follow that criterion while dressing.

- **Never apologize to end the toxic relationship.**

You kept yourself ahead. And you did the right! When you are not happy with that person, or you feel like you are in a cage and it is affecting your mental health. Then buddy! This is not the right person for you. The true relationship is where you both grow together. You both are happy; both are loyal to each other. And if all this is not happening and you are just wasting your life then it is not worth it! Never apologize for building a wall when you were protecting yourself. The right person will always see through them.

- **Never apologize for who you are.**

Why be sorry for what you are? If you have done a mistake or broken someone's heart, if you have not done right to anyone then you can apologize but do not apologize for what you are. You are magic do not apologize for the fire in you. Do not be a people pleaser, you should be confident about who are and see the best in yourself. To appreciate yourself in words and remind yourself of your uniqueness. No matter what happens, no matter how bad it gets but never apologize for being who you are. you do not need to fix yourself you are already perfect just as you are.

Embrace the beauty in you and love yourself then the world will look in a better perspective for you. Never say sorry for "who I am" this depicts that you do not respect yourself. and when you do not respect yourself and how can you expect others to respect you?

3 things you need to improve in your life

- You get angry quickly.

Control anger before it controls you!

Anger is a completely normal, usually healthy, human emotion. But when it gets out of control and turns destructive, it can lead to problems—problems at work, in your personal relationships, and in the overall quality of your life. Anger does not solve anything it builds nothing, but it can destroy everything.

- You waste your whole day because of someone.

When someone gives you bad words or says anything to you. You think about what people will think about you and what will they feel. And because of that 20-30 sec, you are wasting your whole day thinking about that thing. It does not matter what society thinks or what opinion they have of you in spite of that it matters what you think of yourself and how much you respect yourself. **Life is made by your destiny is changed by you not by what others think about you.** So, stop getting frustrated and wasting your whole day due to some creeps and learn to ignore and love yourself.

V

Distract From Distraction

Keep your home screen clean

When your open your mobile. Your biggest enemy is your mobile screen. Android screens easily get messy when you download certain things on them. And basically, it distracts you. The home screen is your starting point of access all the features on your phone. So, the more you keep it clean, the more you will be staying away from distractions.

When you swipe your home screen or open it with your face ID many apps scream- "open me, open me." The mind says the same and you turn to an application where you get the most pleasure it might be Instagram or YouTube. Due, to a lack of awareness and goal of seeing mobile you end up opening one of the apps and spending hours in mindless scrolling. Focus and awareness about the intention come when no app smashes into your face from your home screen and you get some time to go specifically there where you have the work instead of distracting by the other apps. Below is the screenshot of my home screen.

The urge for cleanliness and perfection in arrangement came naturally to me. So, since I got the mobile, I made a separate section for my apps and those sections are there at the bottom of the home screen. This has kept me away from distractions and given me an advantage over most people of my age. And patently, made me the right person to write this book. Following are the point for how I arranged my mobile applications.

08:45
Tue, 03 January
No data

- First section is "More Apps." This section contains applications that are inbuilt into system are rarely or not at all used by me. Thus, I never open this section. It contains Dream League Soccer as well, the only game that I play. I need it only when my mind is flooded with ideas, and I need some healthy distractions to calm it. The game helps me at that time; thus it too is rare and goes into the More Apps section.
- Second section is "Tools." Here, I keep the applications that are not used often, but not that rarely as well. These apps are inbuilt into the system and are simple. These apps do not distract you due to their simplicity and express their soul-purpose of serving you. Some of these apps are- a calculator, contact diary, radio, scanner, screen recorder, VPN, and compass.
- Next, the third, section is "In Use Apps." This section has the apps that I use daily like Email, Video editor, Camera, Notes, LinkedIn, and WhatsApp. As I am not distracted by YouTube and Instagram but use it daily to upload content and research, I kept them in this section too. However, if you are distracted by such apps, then do not keep them in this section even if you use them daily for productive work too. So, where will you keep these? This is the next section.
- Fourth section is "Important Apps." Here, I keep the apps that are not used daily but are frequently important. Such apps consist of Amazon, IQ Option, 991EX calculator, Zoom, and Adobe Acrobat. In the case, where you cannot keep apps in the "In Use Apps" section, you will add those apps here in the fourth section.
- Last, The fifth section. This is called "Google." Here are all my google applications. Apps like Google, Chrome, Snapchat, Google photos, and Gpay are not in frequent use and run on internet. Thus, these have different section.

The above sections highly depend on my lifestyle and timely requirements. These sections can be different for a different people. Assume that you work in a media company then all the media apps like Snapchat, Instagram, Chrome, News, Email, and LinkedIn will be in one section. Thus, either you follow my sectioning criteria or make your own sections using the same fundamentals.

If your phone does not have this sectioning feature, use the following points.

- Keep the apps that are extremely useful for you like contacts, music, and emails at the bottom.
- Your phone must have 1 such app that is useful and keeps you away from distractions which could be a meditation app.
- All else apps, keep it on screen 2 and screen 3.
- Keep it in groups so that it will be easy for you to access it.

Even this small step can increase intense focus in your life

Use a time blocker app if you tend to waste time

When you sit free and when you take a mobile in your hand and open certain social media applications, you surely will waste 1-2 hours browsing it.

For example, if you open Instagram with the thought that you will spend 10-15 min on it, but it happens differently only. You will never know how 10-15 min gets converted into 1- 2 hours. And how you are addicted to it. So, the best way to avoid this is to use a time blocker app.

Time blocker apps allow you to either block or whitelist websites while reminding you of your goals. The single-task nature of time blocking can improve productivity by as much as 80%. You can easily focus for an hour or two at a time and perform work deeply. With time blocking, your schedule becomes your touchstone and eliminates the need to decide what you should focus on.

"Most of us spend too much time on what is urgent and not enough time on what is important." Besides, time blocking also increases your working pace. It follows Parkinson's Law: "The work expands to fill the time slot allotted for its completion." That is why here you fix a specific time (a shorter time slot is recommended) and try your best to complete your work in that time frame.

These are the apps you can use for time blocking: -

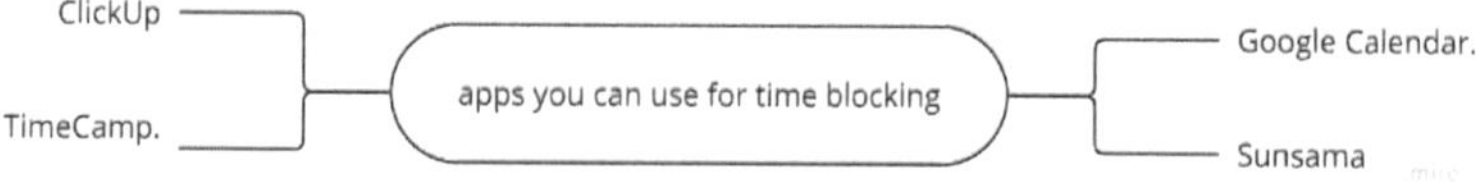

Mute all notifications

Imagine you are in a meeting and suddenly a message pops up with a loud notification tune. Won't it distract or startle you? Of course, yes! Notifications are a way to connect to the apps which you do not need at that time and this way is called distraction.

Just switch off your notifications of all apps. when you see the count on the icon of the app let's say WhatsApp has 12 msg pending, then you may set a time and only check the phone with full focus and awareness in that time.

Notifications are good but becomes one of the worst feature of smartphone if the user is unaware and distracted. Simply turning them off allows you to reduce your phone addiction while still having access to all the apps you use. Without notifications, you are in control of when you pick up your phone, rather than your phone shouting for your attention.

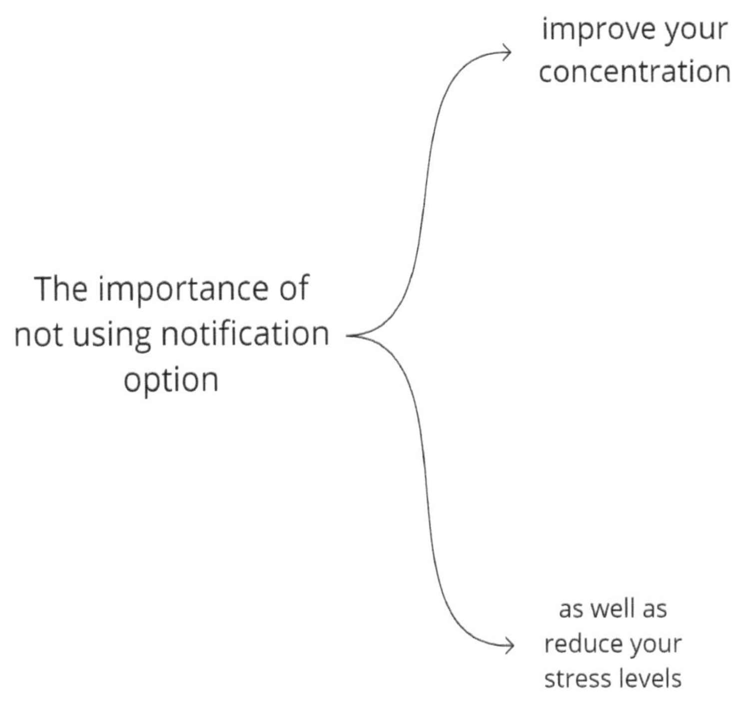

Enter Caption

Start your morning slowly

When you start your morning then instead of checking the phone and replying to everyone just look at yourself, give love to yourself, hug yourself, and say words of kindness to yourself. Start your daily morning with fresh air with a glass of water in your hand and spend time with yourself. When you give yourself the time you will be aware of what to do in a further day and will be staying motivated for the rest of the day. **Silence is the most powerful thing**. When you wake up try to stay silent and analyze yourself.

You may start your morning with morning gratitude which will help you to stay positive and fresh. As per the GIVER ritual you learned in the previous chapter, Make 10 "different" gratitude each day. Do not write and use the same gratitude lines. Feel and say them, then, in that high-vibration state, drink your magic water. What is magic water? See chapter 10.

Getting up and doing exercise will keep you healthy and away from diseases. I am not forcing you to invest 1-2 hours in exercising. I have the same problem. Most of my work needs my brain to be sharp, quick, and focused. But, as I said in the previous chapters that physical workout is the best way to get an extraordinarily powerful mind, we all need to move our bodies. However, I could not give these many minutes in exercising due to the amount of daily work I do. Yet, I get done with my body and mind in less than 1 hour. How? I observed that when my body moves my mind moves. The best example of this is that when you discuss something important with a person or on a call while walking around, your discussion goes to the next level. Your, mind spites out ideas quickly, you are quick to use vocabulary, and you speak, think, and act absolutely great. Why is that? This is because your body is in movement, thus your mind is working exceptionally. This is one of the reasons why you cannot sit quietly and start moving around when your mind is full of thoughts. Here, your brain is moving thus body too moves. The reason why teachers do not teach while sitting and motivational speakers do not speak without moving around the stage is the same. Thus, **A 20-minute intense jog, 6-12 Surya namaskar, and optional breathing and meditation will make your day. And doing it every day will make your life.**

If not with morning exercise, you may do meditation and Wim-Hof breathing separately later in the day. When you do not check devices and give yourself time this is the best growth you are doing.

Do not go directly into work mode, just feel the fresh air. Just enjoy the beautiful weather. Just be grateful for this wonderful life you got. Just look into yourself and see how happy you are! How lucky you are to get this extraordinary life! Just feel blessed and happy for all that you have got.

These all-good habits will keep you focused and goal oriented. And most importantly focused. Tratak is one of the best options to work specifically on your eyesight and focus.

But, in the end, if you are so keen on getting extraordinary success, do not get stuck into these general good habits of feeling the air and getting fresh and all. You know your task and work, do the 30-minute routine I talked about, bathe, and get to your work. A healthy lifestyle is not an option if you are keen to become unstoppable and successful. Read the ninth chapter to know more about what exactly a healthy lifestyle is and why it keeps people average.

Find your max energy time

Max period level means you are at the high point of the level, your brain is working very quickly, ideas are popping up in your brain, and you feel positive and fresh. You have that desire to work on your task and achieve your goals. When do you feel this peak level of energy? For some people, it might be day and for others night. When you realize the max energy period of your day you can manage the task and work efficiently without getting distracted and feeling boredom.

The max energy period for me is night. So, I basically do this like the thinking part, thinking of new ideas, and creating an invention. As the energy is at a high level so the work is done quickly and effectively. And in the morning, I do reading, writing and all. So, it is upon you; which part of the day you like and feel energetic. When you categorize things, you will be more focused things will be clarified in your mind and the task too will be done effectively.

By managing your energy instead of your time, you can not only become more productive but also more fulfilled in your work. You are in a better position to accomplish your goals when you are not overworked and exhausted. Though I know my max energy time of the day, I do not wait until the time comes and eat the big frog first i.e.. do the harder task first. Important tasks come first as well in my list. When you are striving for extraordinary success, you cannot make excuses and this high-energy period should not be your priority at all. Patently, your productivity and work speed and quality are going to differ, but discipline is the key, and you need to work as decided. Discipline is the biggest key. If you have discipline, you do not have to follow any rituals and stuff to be productive and achieve your goal. You will be perfectly unstoppable. However, at first, you need to follow certain things and the max energy period is one of them. So, learn and apply it and become unstoppable to develop a high level of discipline to become more unstoppable.

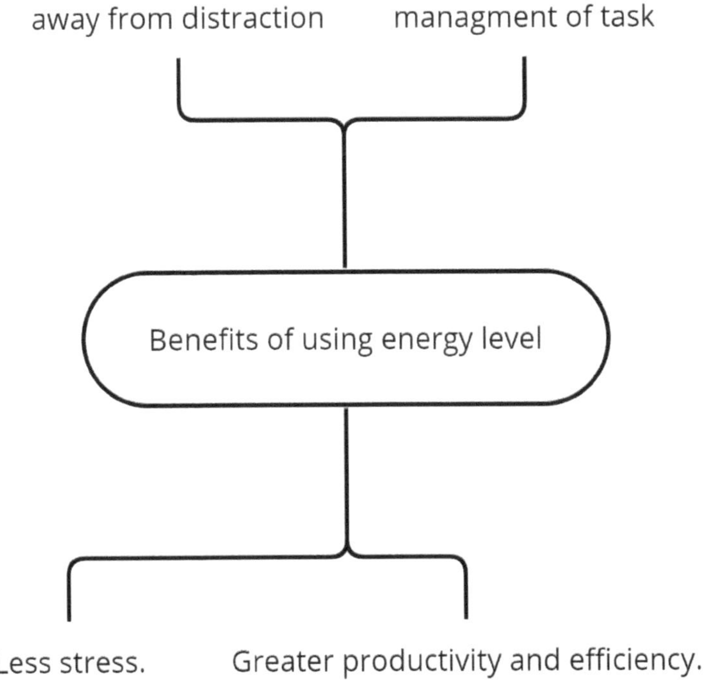

Enter Caption

Pomodoro technique

The Pomodoro Technique is a time management method for students, perfectionists, and procrastinators of all kinds. This technique encourages people to work with the time they have—rather than against it. Using this method, you break your workday into 25-minute chunks separated by five-minute breaks. These intervals are referred to as Pomodoro.

You will get this app easily in androids. Why using this app? You will be more focused completing tasks and away from distractions.

A simple step-by-step method for using the Pomodoro Technique the next time you schedule a work session:

- Identify the task at hand. ...
- Set a timer for 25 minutes. ...
- Take a five-minute break. ...
- Repeat the process three more times. ...
- After the fourth Pomodoro, take a long break. ...
- Repeat the full cycle as needed.

You will be getting some breaks in this technique which is called Pomodoro break. So here are some things you can do in the break.

Things You may Do During Your Pomodoro Break

- Go for a short walk. i.e. – exercise.
- Invest time in mindfulness.
- Get into origami.
- Listen to your favorite playlist.
- Doodle (or draw if you can).
- Have a good stretch.
- Drink some water.

Restrict your information source

We all live in the information zenith age. The give and take of the information is the base of today. However, improper use of it is destroying your mind and body. Stop draining energy on unwanted information that is just filling your brain with waste that later becomes the brain-garbage. Pieces of information from various sites. So, it is better to keep limited sources on which you can rely.

Some information is fake so choose the source from where you can get the correct information and move on with it.

When you get information from various sites you get confused about what you should trust. So, keep limited sources it might have a lot of those resources, but the quantities are NOT infinite. You may mark bookmark on that site which you want, and you may open that frequently.

But be clear on what source you want and at what time. This will keep you away from distractions and make you more focused.

Like in the morning you make take your daily news and in the whole day, your work news and all so be clear on what you should get at what time.

Set up a distraction time

Do you know why Pav Bhaji is your favorite food? Or if you are in America, why that nicely cooked well fried dipped in spice lovely steak seems delicious to you? If you are speaking about the taste, then why a Ferrari is worthy? Why do so many people want to buy buggaty? Now you surely not eat these cars. So, the answer is not taste of food or any of your favorite music. It is just the unavailability of that thing. Everyone in the world say you to cover your body, but what if all will encourage all else to walk naked? Porn will be an extinct concept.

Look, people tend to do things that are more specifically chosen by them and not imposed by others or forcefully done by themselves as well. This is the main reason of you scrolling social media or maybe even a porn site and wasting your valuable time to it. Now here is an activity. Eat only pav bhaji for an entire week or more. Listen to the same song every day for the rest of the week or more. (Time to do the activity...............)

Congratulations for completing the activity. Needless to say, pav bhaji is not your favorite food anymore now you surely love that same green vegetable that you hated. Patently, also, your favorite song has been changed as well. I call it "The Magic of Excessive

Availability."

You see, you are distracted by what you call distraction because you believe it is bad. Once you made it normal, it is going to fade away in the blink of an eye. Ok, I agree that was too much now! But the concept is surely true. And this normalcy lies in the habit of prioritizing your distraction. This does two things. First is that you distract yourself as per the discipline thus you follow discipline and become disciplined. Second, you are prioritizing your bad habits for a specific period so your brain is losing interest and fascination regarding that thing. The same discipline you build can be now used to complete productive tasks as well. So, hurray! you have your productive task done without getting distracted because the distraction itself is in your control. If you want, you may destroy it completely too.

Now, the concept is simple! You will be distracting yourself at your will. Here is where distraction time comes in, where you do anything distracting, but productive. Take the 25-5 minutes rule, for instance, productivity for 25 mins and strictly non-productive for 5 mins. Similarly, you may set an entire day, I call it intoxication day. Here you just be distracted take wine and do a lot of unproductive things. It is strictly prohibited to be productive. Believe me, it is hard. And then you have detoxication day where you just do productive things. Non-productive activities are prohibited. Why are you still reading this book? Go try it make your plan and set up a time quickly. Chop chop!!!

Keep a journal for thoughts

Due to good observation skills and a constant need of thinking, I get many random ideas and observations. Even a thing as simple as burning an essence stick from the lamp seemed magical and unobvious to me once. I keep on discussing many of my observations and ideas with mom and colleagues. However, I did not know why all suggested me the same thing. But now I do.

Keeping a journal helps me a lot in managing my ideas and working on them at a right time. I jot down my every idea in my journal and stop stressing about that. This allows me to focus on my present work with utmost productivity while also generating value in other areas. Now, this is my way of using a journal, but there are many other ways a journal can be used for. One of these ways is as the distraction savior.

You may write your goals and your to-do list just to not get distracted. You can keep your distraction journal in the place where you work and when you feel the urge to take your mobile in your hand. You will be writing down what got you distracted while working on your task/project and how much time you procrastinated. They can be both internal distractions like random thoughts resurfacing in your mind or external ones like notifications on your, smartphone. Make a habit of writing these down as regularly as possible. The more you are able to get thoughts down on paper, the clearer your mind will become, the more aware it will make you of your thoughts and brain functionality, and you will be able to focus better on the tasks you are working on.

Here, it is important to address that thought need not be crapy to be distracting. Any thought that is different from your current task is a distraction. And I have a lot of distracting thoughts as I have my start-up, social media content, and astronomy study too along with this book. Now with these many irrelevant thoughts, it will be a waste of time to write them in a journal. Hence, I prepared a method of deep breathing. Whenever an irrelevant thought arises, I take a deep breath and get back to work or slap myself. Some say it is getting hard on oneself, but it should be understood that your mind is your child, and you must go hard on it to discipline it.

Do not be ashamed of writing down your distractions. Be as honest as possible. This is just for you and your productivity. Once you get stuff down in your Distraction Journal, you can later analyze ways to reduce or eliminate those distractions for the next project or... even work on them later (Yes, you might sometimes have a eureka moment out of the blue).

Takeaway: Maintaining a Distraction Journal (either Physical or Digital) can help you stay focused on your current job and give you an opportunity to get back to your distractions later and compromise on neither productivity nor your distracting thoughts. Also, journal need not be written only, you may do journaling by recording your thoughts or use some other method too.

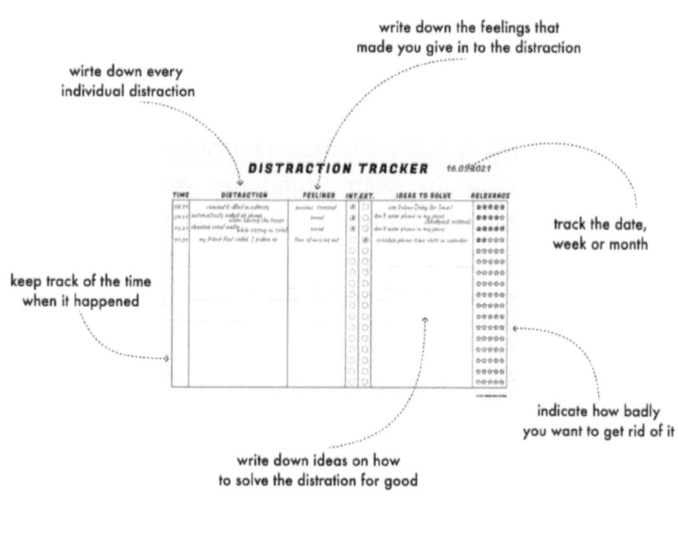

Maintain a routine for yourself

The best way to stay healthy from outside and inside is to maintain a routine. Earlier, I was in a confused state finding the answer to some deep life questions. I remember waking up at 11 AM, getting fresh, starting my routine till the afternoon, and eating at an uneven time. Were those good days for me? Did I feel more positive day by day? Day went productive as I used to work with dedication, but was that satisfactory? The answer to all is "NO."

This uneven, uncertain, and unhealthy routine made me feel boredom, weak, and uneasy which caused lack of focus. So, to avoid this situation and this uneasy routine I maintained a short, nice, and healthy routine. I do not get up early in the morning. It takes me around 5 to 6 AM to get out of bed now. But, if you are a morning bird and able to do so, **Get up early in brahma muhurta**. This is said and experienced to be the best time according to the ancient Indian culture. Brahma muhurta is the morning period between 3.30 a.m. and 5.30 a.m. It is suitable for meditation. After a good night's sleep, the mind is refreshed, calm and serene.

Doing daily yoga will help you to activate your chakras and help you to get a healthy life. Getting up and drinking some water and starting your day with a huge smile makes a fresh start to the day. Maintaining a routine will make you disciplined and will help you to keep yourself away from distractions.

As per explained earlier in a few chapters making a daily schedule and following it keeps you in work mode which makes you more focused and makes your day productive. It also helps to keep you away from anxiety, and stress, and hyperactivity that are the reasons of distraction.

This will help you to get more dedicated to your goals and to achieve them.

So always make a routine and work on it.

"You cannot do big things if you are distracted by small things"

VI

Harsh Truth Of Relationships

You will outgrow your friends

You might have heard teachers say this when you were in school: "all friendships last only until you finish your final exam, then after everything starts to go in different directions and no one will stick by you." Every student, at that time, may have taken it as nonsense. They say- "we are friends forever. We are made for each other. We will do everything together and be successful together." But, when it actually hits life, you learn the hard truth. "It is all an illusion, I should better focus on myself and my life," your mind screams. It is common to grow out of certain friendships, especially when your lives diverge. You will face many promises from your friends of staying together and long-lasting friendships, but it is all fake. People frequently discover that their childhood, high school, or even college plans are less like their plans as they get older.

A few days back, I caught up in a conversation with Raj. He is currently employed by the government and receives better pay. He explained to me how friends may do both "good and terrible" things in life when we first met and talked about his life. He met his buddies while working toward his 12th degree, and they later evolved into his so-called "family friends". Raj was an extremely bright and gifted kid who consistently received top grades throughout his school journey. As soon as he made friends, he began to be drawn to the new direction in which his companions traveled, such as spending time on the grounds, abandoning classes, traveling, etc. Due to all these things, he lost concentration and ultimately decided to take a job rather than achieve his goal of becoming a well-known big officer. This concludes that it is better for you and your future to let go of such friends who are not adding any value to your life.

Here is an activity for you -You should list the names of two people who are close to you and share your values. Also, write down the values you share.

And it is okay to outgrow friends! You are no longer the same set of friends you lost. your habits and all have changed. Do not feel bad if you outgrow your friends when you are trying to become a better person. Do not let them hold you back from growing into a better person. Sometimes your friends want to stay in that bad environment, but you need to walk out leaving them behind. A rocket cannot fly high with a lot of weight on it, a ship cannot sail carrying excessive weight, and similarly, a human cannot achieve higher success with a lot of companions. Choosing people wisely is an art because you need to choose a few of them to keep with you.

Rashi was waiting for her companions to return from mathematics lectures on the first day of college as she sat on the campus. In the green beauty and a small crowd of students, she made some new acquaintances and met new folks for her class. "I am going to live my college life to the fullest; parties, boys, drugs, travel, and a lot of fun;" Tina said as she entered the university cafeteria and began chatting with Rashi. Rashi enrolled in the course with a vision and objective in mind since she was committed to achieving her goals. Over a few days difference between the worldview of Tina and Rashi outgrew Tina from Rashi's life. Many people will try to lead you down the wrong path and sabotage your future. So, it would be best to let these people go. It is important to subtract things for good as it is to add them.

Few people will suck your energy

I used to have some mates who would call anytime and take 1 hour easily without any serious reason. These people get bored with their own state and want someone else to accompany them in their boring life. I call them Energy suckers. Energy sucker is not only those who take your time, but also who take your vibes. As social creature, we tend to live with a group of people, where we forgot to calculate the aftermath of the situation. Energy drainers or energy suckers can be social media, habits, and thoughts too. The people, however, play a major role in triggering your urge to put yourself into the situation of energy drainage.

Some people around you will come into your life who know to drain your energy. Sometime will be there in your life when the person who is in front of you is just sucking your energy and depending upon you, and not creating their own energy. It is better to stay away from this relationship. This will affect you in a very harsh way.

Energy drainers are those things that we are tolerating, ignoring, or putting up with that are draining us of our precious energy. Energy Drainers can be mental or physical clutter and when they are handled, you can reclaim the energy that is being used up by them. So, if you think someone is draining your energy, pay attention to your ability to focus and remember things when you are surrounded by them, or immediately after you have talked with them. If it feels like your IQ has magically dropped by 20 points, that is clearly a warning sign.

Speaking about the short, frequent, or rare conversations, one must remember that they are like business meetings that decides the growth of the company and the company is your life. You should decide on a time slot for your meeting. I use 15 minutes. In these 15 minutes, try to listen as much as you can and just ask questions with an expectation of answers. This is the way to find if the conversation is adding some value to you and your life. If you get satisfactory answers to your question, then continue with the conversation, else leave. The most important part of leaving the conversation is the ability to say no and that has been explained in previous chapters. If it still feels rude then you may follow the given method. So, the moment the second person stops telling you appreciate the person or belonging of him/her. After the appreciation, you continue the sentence and let the person know that you will leave for now and will meet him/her later. Remember, while informing about leaving, you should already be stepping out of the zone instead of standing there and never looking back once you left. This method will not make the second person feel rude and gets you out of the energy-draining and time-consuming conversation.

"The same people who are candy to your eyes can be a poison to our hearts. Study the ingredients before feeding them to your soul." Pay attention to whom your energy increases and decrease around because that is the universe is giving you a sign to stay away from. Become more aware of what really your energy is worth.

People inspire you or they drain you, so always remember to choose them wisely. Energy helps you to stay focused and it is the most important aspect of spirituality.

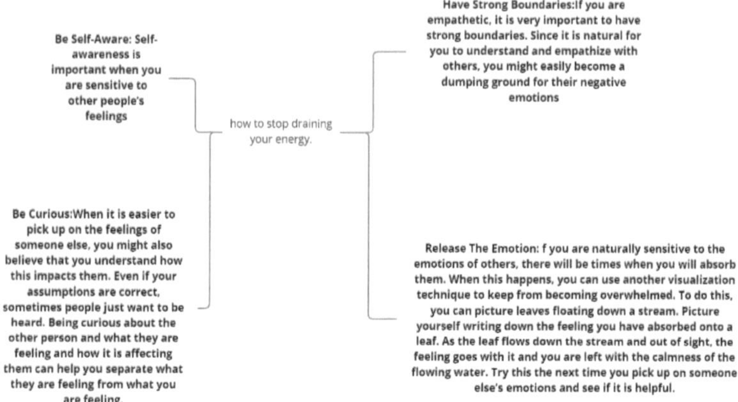

Sometimes people would not love themselves

Have you ever noticed the behavior of an army man? He is always so disciplined and thinks the same for others too. The discipline that he develops in himself becomes the thing that he seeks in others two. Why do saddhus never hate any person and are ready to help those in need? They are fulfilled and blissful among themselves. These people love the self and that is what goes into the world as well.

You see, when you are proud of yourself because you are achieving valuable goals in your life and gaining significance for your work, you love the work and treat the people with love and respect too. No one can make you sad in that state, thus it is also called a high-vibration state. Nevertheless, as you treat yourself well, you treat others well and get fame and positive attention. Thus, self-love increases, and it gets us more success and so on. This graph goes on increasing from there on, until we choose to go on a low-level frequency due to few critics. The people who do not value themselves will never be valued by society. Thus, it is important to seek a way to develop self-love and self-respect before loving others.

You should always make yourself powerful and valued. The more you think good about yourself the more society will think good about you. Respect yourself and the same will be given to you by others.

There is a trick you may use to refresh yourself after a moment of hating or self-doubting. Just hug yourself by putting your hands around your body. And talk to yourself. Apologize to yourself using sorry, praise yourself using thank you, and express the feeling of gratitude for what you have achieved and motivate to go ahead. With a few deep breaths and a smile on your face, end this self-talking session.

"People who love themselves, do not hurt others. People who are fulfilled always think about the growth of the other too."

Choosing a life partner is the most important decision

If you choose to have a partner in life, whoever you choose is probably the most important decision you make. So, when you look forward to your future, make sure you are with the person whom you love. I have seen many cases in the current world, where couples marry each other but they are not able to stay in that relationship and end up with a divorce.

The root cause of most fights, arguments, and divorces is miscommunication. Assuming and presuming comes hand in hand with this issue. Family issues and financial burdens- if not discussed- lead to separation and divorce. They can be hideous as well. It will influence your happiness, career success, health, finances, children, friends, and family. So, it is not a decision you want to take lightly. Choosing someone that brings out the best in you and adds a sense of joy and ease to your life is essential to your emotional and physical well-being. Who you marry, which is the ultimate partnership, is enormously important in determining the happiness in your life and your success.

When you are with the best partner you both grow together, conquer the world together, and build your beautiful empire. Imagine you are with your partner and you both are well settled, have your own house, and travel in your personal jet. Isn't this wonderful to imagine? Then, think it is going to be real. How good it would feel? When you are with the best person everything that you dreamed of gets fulfilled. You never understand a person in 2 or 3 meets. It sometimes takes years to understand one. So, do not be in a hurry and take your life decision in just a few seconds or a few days. Take your time and see who is best for you. After all, your life is decided by this one decision.

The relationship that you share with your life partner is the one meant to last forever, a relationship that is permanent in your life (at least that is what most people want it to be like at the time of getting married). Even though one might say that you spend the maximum part of your day with your colleagues or business partners, they do not have as much of an influence on your personal life, decisions, and career choices.

Having a supportive life partner becomes all the most important today because the market is more volatile than ever before, mergers and acquisitions are rampant, and job types frequently change. You never know when your boss might change, your organization might experience a cultural drift, your projects might change, and you get laid off because of cost-cutting, and so on. At some point, you might think of moving your job, trying some management roles, changing career path, or even pursuing higher studies.

Amidst all these challenging and crucial milestones in your career trajectory, if you get a life partner who supports you and understands your career challenges, dreams, aspirations, and priorities your life partner will become a support system.

To all those married people, make sure you are as supportive and considerate of your partner's choices. Value and support your partner unconditionally, but also make sure that you do not lose out on yourself in the process. Offer unconditional support and love to your life partner but make sure that you are also not leaving yourself behind. Only if you have something in abundance can you radiate that to your environment.

When you are happy and satisfied, you will make others and your environment happier. Even if one person is unhappy and dissatisfied, the relationship can topple. Lastly, if you are unmarried, give 10 times thought to understand how much you're to-be life partner will understand your career choices, the challenges attached to it, future decisions, commitments, priorities, dreams, and aspirations. Go for a life partner who considers your dreams and choices as his own, pushes you to achieve more, and lifts you up in case of failures.

Your marriage as well as your career can go hand in hand if you back your partner and at the same time back yourself too to keep the wheels of marriage healthy, strong, and stable.

VII

7 Wonderful Habits

Read everyday

I heard my teacher once saying- "leaders are readers." Is it true? Hundred percent. It feels like yesterday when I started reading. In 8th class, I caught a sudden attraction towards reading. Though I continued reading different books throughout my childhood, I developed a genuine interest in books to make it my hobby and habit. In ninth class, I got my first two books, from which, I feel I started my journey of becoming an author at an early age. It was my state-level soccer tournament at CST, Mumbai. We played our game and the tournament ended. While leaving the city, the team stopped by a shop to buy Cristiano Ronaldo's number 7 jersey of Juventus. He was newly transferred into Juventus that year, so it was the craze to buy that jersey for us players and fans. All my mates were buying jerseys. Meanwhile, I, here, was not in that shop. Where was I? I was in the neighboring shop looking for two books to buy. And lo! I got my first self-help book- "Who says you can't, you do" and my first extraordinary science book- "A brief history of time." I used to read and apply the knowledge every day. The fact that I chose to study astrophysics is an example of my dedication to books. A brief history of time showed me this dream. And I started my personal development journey from that book. Still, I went through many trials and errors. Nevertheless, the point of this story is that I started reading books in the ninth class and wrote my own book and published too in twelfth. A revision book of astronomy and astrophysics is my first book that I published merely three years after reading. This shows how powerful the reading is and how quickly it transforms you.

Reading books changed my life. reading Is one of the extremely valuable habits that you can develop. And, believe me, once you are in, there is no getting out. It helped and constantly helped me think in the most unique ways and make the impossible things possible if I want them to be possible.

Besides abstract development, reading has numerous practical benefits. An increment in creativity and imagination is one of those benefits. Reading is the best habit that you can inculcate in yourself and do miracles. Successful people say at least complete 100 books before you turn "30". However, I recommend reading one book per month and gradually increasing it to two, three, and so on gives the best Return on Investment. When you read a book, your brain gets wired. You get to know new things. Some people may have difficulty developing the habit of reading. How to develop a mindset for reading?

Even though I feared reading, I somehow managed to read textbooks. The only thing people can read is newspapers because they are small and do not consume a lot of time and attention.

You may use this technique to read the books:

- Choose a book wisely: Read what you want and what benefits you and not just because someone else is reading/ recommending that.
- Small portion at a time: Write a note on the back page of the table of contents you are reading.

    - Plan each weekday.
    - Day 1 - pages 1 to 10

    - Day 2- pages 11 to 24
    - Day 3- pages 25 to 30

- Allocation of these portions is not arbitrary. It is done in a manner that logical breaks are introduced in between.
- Reading a book is a marathon long not a sprint. Do not try to read fast so that you can reach to finish line. Read at the pace where you will understand the paragraphs.
- Conquer ½ short books first: read small books first and make yourself comfortable. Once you got that habit of reading you may start reading big books.

Do you know how Mt. Everest was conquered? By capturing small peaks one after another. Remember, reading fictional books is the same as watching a movie. Thus, avoid fictional books unless you want to be a fictional book writer. Instead, choose a non-fictional book related to your field, like I chose A brief history of time, then Six easy pieces, then theory of relativity, and some self-development books like the psychology of money, Think and grow rich, Elon Musk, Rich dad poor dad, and The subtle art not giving a F*ck.

At first, decide a specific time period to give into reading like reading 30-35 minutes every day. Later, as you progress, read by chapters, like complete 1 chapter of this book today. Reading early in the morning is said to help you get clear on your thought and get your brain back into proper momentum. But you may read anytime in a day. I prefer to read whenever I got bored by the same work or irritated due to a minor disturbance in work or when I am literally not doing anything. **And congratulations to you for completing this book till here. You are becoming a pro reader day-by-day!**

Meditate everyday

Meditating for at least 10 minutes everyday possess the potential to transform a huge part of your profession and personal life for good. The person who does not exercise at all sees the result of exercise at the fastest pace and most prominently. Similarly, if you do not meditate at all, start with 10 minutes a day, then gradually increase it and if you are already a meditator go and increase your meditation time and quality. The quality and quantity of meditation depend upon several factors. Position, breathwork, concentration, and willpower. If I talk about us, I prefer to sit in the Lotus posture (*padmasana*) and Kshitija- Easy pose (*Sukhasana*). Easy pose is the most practiced pose throughout the world. In fact, in India, we sit in the Easy pose for consuming our daily meals. I prefer to use Wim-Hof breath work which is explained in the 10th chapter. Besides, the time for meditation matters a lot too. For most people and recommended-by-culture-time is in the morning or early in the morning (*Brahma-muhurta*). However, for me, it is night time. Night-time is also an excellent time to meditate. Aghoris and great shiva-yogis meditate at night when all the radiation ends, and supernatural entities become powerful to allow us to gain different experiences. It is said that super-natural entities can be felt in the night time meditation. It seems unbelievable, but I had many such experiences where I experienced the presence of supernatural entities during meditation at night and before 5:30 in the morning on the terrace. It is not true that these entities only stay at haunted places like in the movies; Some of them might be reading this book with you sitting beside you.

The point is; besides a beneficial act, meditation is a journey of a seeker. The journey- full of ups and down as you will never get the same experience. The journey- full of thrill as the experience can lead you to another dimension and extreme conditions of sorrow and bliss at the same time. The journey that never ends but keeps on displaying its ultimate and infinite possibilities.

Do you know why we feel the presence of energies while meditating? You get more aware of your surrounding and yourself. In physicality, the minute you are distracted, you will realize that you have work to do. This awareness never let me fall in the trap of distraction which is the case with today's young generation. I am always aware of my distraction, and I constantly thrive and find ways to get out of that state. Sometimes I keep myself terribly distracted for an entire day, but the good point is that it is a willing decision and done with complete awareness. This also is an activity and develops you to a higher level. Here, we develop ourselves by following all our bad habits and dropping ourselves into a terrible state willingly to realize the worst results of it and start a fresh positive journey out of that rage and regret. Nevertheless, I will talk about that topic later.

Some of the meditation's theorized benefits are self-control, objectivity, tolerance, enhanced flexibility, equanimity, improved concentration and mental clarity, emotional intelligence, and the ability to relate to others and oneself with kindness, acceptance, and compassion. Meditation can produce a deep state of relaxation and a tranquil mind. This process may result in enhanced physical and emotional well-being.

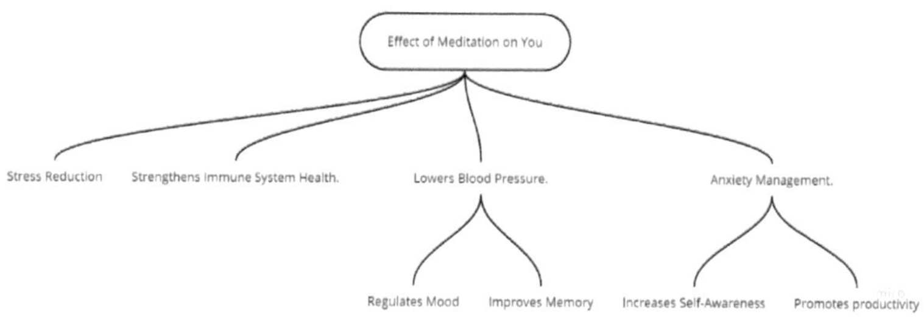

Workout 6 days/week

Though we talked about exercise and working out a lot in previous chapters, it is worth writing a reminder short paragraph about it.

Adding exercise to your routine can positively affect your life. Working out regularly keeps you fit and healthy. It helps you to increase your stamina and your will power. Working out daily will help you to get fresh and look smart. You may even play your favorite game an hour a day and see results in few days. You will feel fresh and lighter. Working out taught us not just self-discipline and self-respect. It has contributed to your growth as a leader. Keep your aim for at least 30 minutes of moderate physical activity every day. If you want to lose weight, maintain weight loss, or meet specific fitness goals, you may need to exercise more. Reducing sitting time is important, too. The more hours you sit each day, the higher your risk of metabolic problems. Exercise strengthens your heart and improves your circulation. The increased blood flow raises the oxygen levels in your body. This helps lower your risk of heart diseases such as high cholesterol, coronary artery disease, and heart attack. Regular exercise can also lower your blood pressure and triglyceride levels.

Benefits of exercise: -

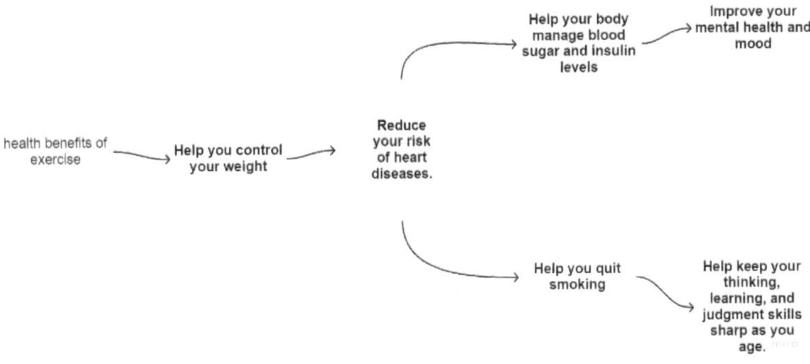

Sleep for 7-8 hours in a day

Sleeping well is perhaps the single biggest determination of physical and mental energy. It is ridiculous how easy it is to gain that energy and how many of us still waste this natural cure to so many problems!

Research says, sleeping for 7-8 hours a day helps your brain to rest and helps to Lower your risk for serious health problems, like diabetes and heart disease.

Sleeping for 7-8 hours daily reduces stress and improves your mood expands your Thinking skills and helps you more clearly and do better in school and at work.

In spite of that, Your mood is fresh and you are happy so because of that it helps you to Get along better with people.

Enough sleep helps your brain to function properly. This can help you to impair your properties. to concentrate, think clearly, and process memories.

If you cannot sleep:

- Set a bedtime routine.
- Limit naps to 20 min.
- Exercise earlier in the day.
- Make your bedtime quiet and dark.
- Avoid electronic material near to the bed.
- Stop screening before 3 hours of sleep.
- Sleep with silence and avoid using devices.

Having said this, I also want you to remember that Elon Musk used to sleep under the desk after hours of coding and next day the same routine while creating X.com- his first startup. So, in the quest for success and fulfillment this healthy and comfortable lifestyle needed to be sacrificed. Yeah, you may follow it later but not now. However, if you are in a job or living an average life, then surely follow this to make your life extraordinary.

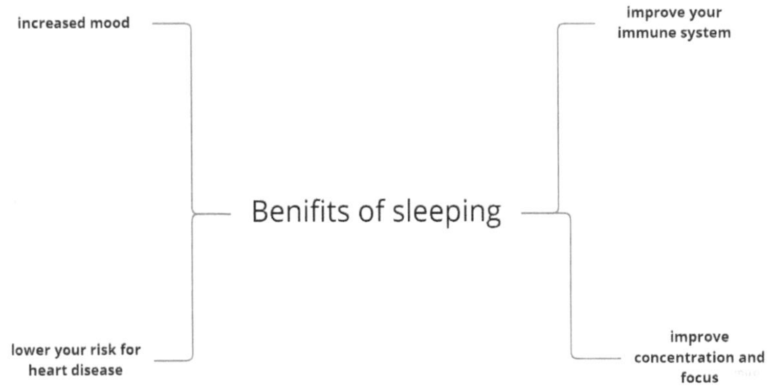

Meet someone new

One of the two best ways people like Elon Musk and Bill Gates learn is through discussion. They do not have to pay expensive fees to colleges in order to learn rocket science. Elon Musk learned rocket building by reading a few books and asking a lot of questions for answers from professionals. You need to have the right question. Suppose you have an exam in a few weeks and a topic is exceedingly difficult to you, just go and find a random person and ask him/her to explain that to you. With social media apps like LinkedIn, you have a greater chance of finding someone for productive purposes and learning. Applications like Cambly are good for speaking skills and learning new languages. Applications like Omegle improve your communication skills and teaches you to talk and deal with strangers.

People have amazing stories, amazing experiences, and amazing things to share. It is like reading a book a week, in less than 30 min. These conversations will teach you many new things and will help you to expand your knowledge and your skill. It is important that you do not become an extrovert but interact with people and learn new things. Also, provide them with solutions to their problems. **"People value those personalities who add value to their personality."**

People pay Lacs of rupees to learn communication, but do you agree that sometimes the best thing is the cheapest? How did Physics Wallah founder- Alakh Pandey- become one of the world's best teachers? Well, he did not pay for any high-valued course because even courses produce only 5 to 10 percent of legend. Alakh Pandey went for help to random people, colleagues, classmates, relatives, friends, and students of his very first tuition class he joined. He asked only two questions- "who was your favorite teacher in school" and "why was the teacher your favorite." He talked to them and surveyed. He marked the results of the conversations and marked the qualities of his favorite teachers he came to know about. Then, he started practicing and inculcating those qualities in himself and applying them in his teaching. Today, by the time I am writing this, He is the founder and CEO of India's 101st unicorn- Physics Wallah.

So, people, this is the power of discussion, meeting, and surveying. It is fun, Productive, affordable, and effective. Now, you know how to meet and why to meet. Hence, I challenge you to learn 3 topics or skills by interacting with people online for free.

No TV at all

One decision of my parents that I thank the most is that they removed the television cable when I was in 7th standard. It was not their decision because of my behavior or addiction to TV, though, I used to watch a lot. They were forced to do so due to complicacy in the set-top box subscription. So, thanks to the universe. In India, when a child reaches 10th and 12th, TV connections are out as children have their boards. But, at my place, I lost the TV in 7th, and we got a bigger LED smart TV in 10th. However, something changed in me. In the absence of TV, I developed something in my personality that I lost my interest in TV and TV shows. I had my goals, shifted to YouTube for learning without random non-personalized ads, and knew the reason why the content of ads is different on TV and YouTube.

You see, the TV informs you about vessel cleaner, washroom cleaner, Honda bike, washing powder Nirma, and Kis mi chocolate. They know what TV is doing to you. It is making you average. They know that the people spending their time on TV do not want a positive change in life, they are average people who clean dishes, clothes, and vessels all their lives with a Hero Honda in their tiny parking. The people who watch TV cannot afford a Ferrari because they are broke and they cannot afford self-development courses because they have no minds and will to change. Do you want to stay in this mess? Are you one of those average broke people who are a liability to humanity?

Less tv means more time feeling alive, more chances of sticking to your schedule, and more time thinking. It is better not to watch serials which have a lot of impact on our minds and thinking. And sometimes those characters come in your dream to haunt you. If you want the results that rich and highly intelligent people have, then go to the platform they are on and consume the information they do. You too will one day see an ad of a Ferrari and buy it.

Sharing what you know, everyday

Sharing connects you with people and marks your existence on this planet. Sharing it with absolute transparency will make you extremely comfortable with whom you are. Sharing the blog and uploading your views on social media will help you to connect with various people. And various perspectives as well. The act of sharing knowledge alone is great for building rapport and relationships, where people get that warm fuzzy feeling from either sharing their wisdom or picking up on the wisdom of others. Sharing knowledge helps them connect, perform better, and become stronger as professionals. Some examples of advantages of knowledge sharing for your organization are that you can save money on training, and capture and keep know-how, even if one day employees decide to work somewhere else.

We recommend uploading 3-5 contents across your all-social media platform. Using social media as a creator will give you a massive success as compared to using it as a consumer. And this massive success needs sharing your hearts with people across the globe. Moreover, sharing highlights your existence, your knowledge, and your contribution to the society.

VIII

Mind's Seven Tricks

Spotlight effect

I still remember when I was in 10th std and as I was in English medium school, so my Marathi was a little bad and we were having a lecture on Marathi going on. Jagtap Ma'am told me to read the passage from the textbook. The number- "78-" was obviously provided in Marathi. Unable to pronounce it in Marathi, I went on reading it in its English name. And soon I was greeted by the laughter of students. At that very time, I felt like all are judging me, and will always remember that. I was worrying about that till my day ended and I realized it is nothing like I thought. No one in the world has time to think about your mistake all lifelong. If it would be the case, then you would be a celebrity. But you are not. This is the perk of not being famous. So, you need to have patience and remember that you are not the center of anyone's life.

The spotlight effect is the psychological phenomenon through which people tend to believe that they are noticed more than they actually are. The reason for the spotlight effect is the innate tendency to forget that although one is the center of one's own world, the person is not the center of everyone else's. This tendency is prominent when one does something atypical.

For example, If Raj is in a meeting and arrives late for some reason. He must, therefore, be concerned about what others will think of him. But the truth is that nobody cares about him. Considering this, overthinking and anxiety are also the results of this tendency. Overthinking directly affects your mental health and you feel negative. The surrounding goes pale and looks depressed.

Each one of us encounters the spotlight effect daily. Anytime you are wearing a dress, the thought must have crossed your mind- how will people perceive your clothing, will they say anything, and so on.

Another situation that comes to mind is when you rush to work and had untidy hair. You would believe that everyone is evaluating you based entirely on your hair, but this is inaccurate. This occurs in those who experience "anxiety" and "stress."

The spotlight effect is thought to result from excessive self-consciousness and an inability to see things from the other person's perspective in order to recognize that their perspective is different from yours. The Spotlight Effect can, however, be controlled with medication and other methods. Greater self-love, acknowledging your worth, and accepting yourself just as you will cure it.

<u>The task for today</u>: -Today, spend some time alone, whether in a room or outside in nature. List the things you fear and give them a thought. Then, try to determine if you have social anxiety. Am I concerned about what people will think? Am I Currently residing on Other People's Terms? And if so, why? Also, tell yourself how you will stop this.

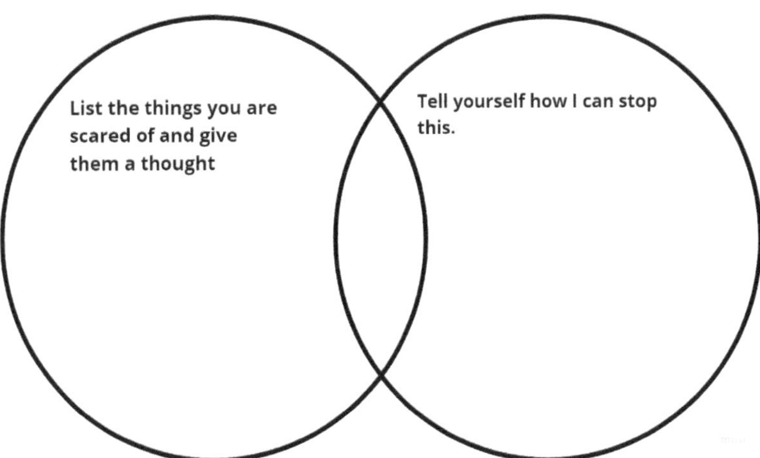
List the things you are scared of and give them a thought
Tell yourself how I can stop this.

Once you discover the solution, you will finally stop searching and begin living. "Living a life that is fulfilled."

The third-person effect

In college, on my first day, we were playing a game. One of the questions was, "How many of you use social media platforms like Instagram and Facebook roughly 12 hours out of 24 hours?" Sir instructed us to answer honestly. This was a recent instance of the third-person effect. None of the 40 students complained that they used it and assumed that "all others use it instead of me."

In a similar context, the Third person effect person's tendency to think that other people are more influenced by mass media than him/her. People tend to believe that they are less influenced by others. When you open a social media application, ask yourself- "have you made a specific time for using any social media app like 15 min a day or 1 hour a day"; "Are you investing your 1 hour on LinkedIn." I said 'investing', not wasting.

However, according to the self-enhancement view, the third-person effect was predicted negative for people. It harms them in a negative way, but the research made it clear now that it is been driven by motivation and self-esteem. Also, people are getting aware that they are getting infused by social media. They are getting aware of how they are wasting their hours by mindless scrolling and consumption of pornography. Due to these habits, the brain suffers an addictive state of dopamine need and pulls oneself into a deep valley of grief, self-doubt, and laziness.

When I spoke to Shyam once, he was worried about his upcoming board exam because he had not studied and was squandering his precious study time on movies. As a result, he lost focus and felt under pressure. He tossed social media out of his life upon my view on the good and bad effects of it. This helped him develop his objective and concentrate.

the third-person effect is not just a media effect perception, as it also seems to have implications for the perception of the influence of other sources of information.

My niece "Tanu" is just 13 years old. but when I ask her about upcoming movies which are going to launch or who is the heroine in that movie. Which movie is this song from? She has all the answers. Today's generation is just fast forward, and they know all the news as they are watching devices. Unlike past generations, today's greed is for information.

When you use the media for good things like genuine learning and content creation it benefits you multifold. The media is the most powerful entity on earth. They have the power to make the innocent, guilty and to make the guilty, innocent. It controls the minds of the masses.

So do not let the media influence you in any way!

Task (write down the answers in the pace given below):

How much time you are using social media.

-

Is it adding value to your life?

-

Are you investing your time or wasting it on social media platforms?

-

Self-analyze yourself and limit the time for it!

Status quo bias

Kiara got a new offer from a company of cable, but she sticks to her current satellite provider even though she might get offers of more channels at a cheaper price.

Status quo bias is people preferring things to stay the same by doing nothing or sticking with the decision made previously. This could happen when only small transition costs are involved, and the importance of the decision is great. Because of the habit of not accepting the changes and growing yourself, one can miss more beneficial options.

Rakhi was a new candidate applying for the computer course. When I discovered that she was aware of a few computer shortcuts, I went over and tried a discussion with her. However, she lost the opportunity because of her propensity for not accepting things since she had a bad attitude and was unable to accept that someone else might know more than her in a particular profession. These people also try to avoid risk generated by chance even when the risk is less than from making no change!

For example, when a company adds new insurance plans to your list of insurance options, you choose the old plan frequently. And not adopting the new changes. When you go to a stationary and when u see many pens but still you take the pen which you are using for years. You should avoid this. You should explore new things instead of sticking to one place. When you do that, you get to know new things and explore new creativity.

It is the general tendency of people to make repeated choices and keep things in order. People avoid change and a simple example would be trying the same food every time and not trying anything new when visiting a specific restaurant.

You will never learn anything new if you only focus on one thing and do not try anything else. Whenever animals figure out the change in the environment they try to migrate from there because maybe it will be easy to catch the predictor in that climate or due to lack of food. "Change is constant" so we should always accept the change and move on.

Rahul was an assistant professor at the NDNVP Institute, but after a year he had an offer for a higher position at Rajasthan University, which he declined because he was happy and well-paid there. He did not want to leave his comfort zone, though, and merely wanted to stay in that position. Your talents improve as a result of gaining new experiences, which also increases your knowledge.

How can you overcome it:

- Accept its existence: the first way to overcome is to accept it, whenever stuck in a situation. People should have a habit to recognize and see if they are taking any decision out of bias and try to change it if needed. For e.g.: When you are going out and someone compliments you on your appearance but says you don't look attractive in this dress, you decide to wear a different dress instead of your favorite. So, beware of this and do not think about what others will say or judge you. At the end of the day Do what your heart says!
- Seek external help: whenever you need to take any decision you may seek any of your friends or if you want advice related to business or personal life you may take advice from an expert opinion which will give you a wider perspective and produce rational thinking. Once, I need a suggestion for my startup and a piece of advice. Instead of instantly working on my plans I took some suggestions from my sir who is also an NLP trainer and an entrepreneur. Which helped me a lot in my future. Similarly, you may seek external help. When I first Rohan we had a great talk regarding spirituality and all and with that, he taught me many stuffs regarding meditation, breathing, yoga, and all so with this you get to know immense information that helps you to grow.

Activity:

Tomorrow, try a new thing like eating a new dish or buying a new thing, or talking to an external person who may help you or advice you. Explore one new thing tomorrow (and write in the below space.)

Zeigarnik effect

You must have experience when we make our to-do list and unfortunately when we fail to complete it our focus goes on the incomplete tasks rather than the complete ones. The Zeigarnik effect is a psychological tendency in which people remember an incomplete task rather than a completed one. This results in greater mental effort and rehearsal in order to keep the task at the forefront of awareness. Once completed, the mind is then able to let go of these efforts.

Whenever I make my to-do list, let us say, of 10 tasks in a day. Sometimes one or two tasks remain incomplete, so my focus used to go on those which were incomplete tasks and not on that I succeeded to complete 8 tasks. And, due to this effect will make you unsatisfied and sometimes lose hope too. Instead of focusing on many tasks, it is better when you focus on one task and give your 100% into it rather than having 8-10 task pressure on you.

Zeigarnik's effect also has a great impact on relations. Knowing that we tend to recall things better when they are unresolved means that we are more likely to recall a break that did not got repaired. This means that we will continue to recall the negative qualities of our partner again and again. "She always tries to hurt me." "He never listens to me."

Once I met Sayli my childhood friend who is a dancer by profession when I met her, we had a chat regarding some stuffs and she started to tell me about her boyfriend, and how he always brings her past into them. And the root cause of fighting and start of misunderstandings. The golden rule of relationships is we should never bring 3 people into our relationship. You cannot give any random person so much importance that he/she came to be the "relation-breaker" between you two.

You might be eager to learn more because the story is unfinished. Another example of the Zeigarnik effect is typically found in education. When I was had exams in school days, teachers used to tell that do not just read the text for the sake of exams keep it in mind "learn-by-heart." But we never took that seriously. And when final exams used to come, we need to again start learning from zero. It's common for students to take exams in school that require studying and cramming before the exam but once the exam is over, they might experience difficulty recalling the information they learned. For this, you need to learn and concentrate from starting and focus on what you are learning and not what others are doing. You may make flow charts and make notes out of them. When you have vision in front of your eyes nothing seems impossible for you

One of my friends experienced this while watching her favorite TV show. At the end of the episode, it ends with a cliff-hanger. She was eager to learn more because the story is unfinished. That is the Zeigarnik effect. Her attention did not go on what happened in entire movie, on the last part that was unfinished. Another example is after a job interview. You may be focused on all the things you perceive as wrong that happened during the interview, rather than the positive points. But after you get hired, all those negative thoughts might fall away as you begin training for a new role. Instead of focusing on the negative side, see its positive side as to what changes should you do in yourself that this will not happen in the next interview.

These are the percentages of how much you remember for finished task and incomplete task.

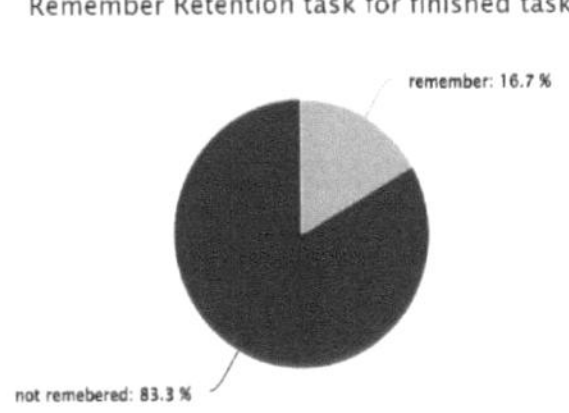

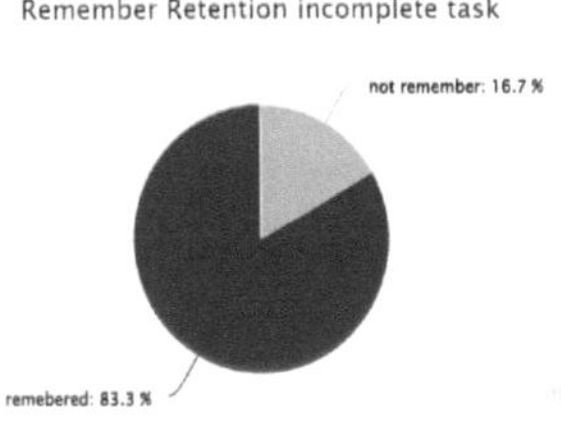

Activity: Make a **6 day challenge** to yourself and before sleeping make a to-do list and try to complete it. And if not then what YOU learned for this day and how you can make changes in yourself focus on that and write in the column

Ikea effect

Once, when Mansi- an excellent artist- made a huge painting for a competition that was held at the state level. Almost 50 students applied, and Mansi thinks that she made the best painting. She started appreciating the painting by herself. Due to the Ikea effect, this happens. But despite of this she may approach new painters and learn new techniques from them or have a conversation with new strangers. This may help her in her future career life. You should always take it in a positive way and move on. Have you ever felt like no one genuinely appreciates your carefully put-together outfits? This effect describes how people tend to value an object more if they make (or assemble) it themselves. More broadly, the IKEA effect speaks to how we tend to like things more if we have expended effort to create them.

When Riya made samosa she asked mom, "How is the samosa? I made it." This proves that she is giving more value to what she made. Instead, she should learn from her mom if there is any mistake and happily accept the advice that mom will give. When you make things of your own and with a lot of effort, obviously you will love it.

Another example is that every parent believes that their child is the best in school. When I used to score well and perform well in class, my parents used to be always proud of me and believed that I am the brightest student in the entire class. But, with this, we should always keep in mind that there are many students in the school who are scoring well and had passed out with good marks. We Must always appreciate them as well.

Whenever you go on a trip to the places that you have explored look amazing to you. Also, when you see the status of people on WhatsApp you always tend to believe that the places you have visited are best than those your neighbor has gone to. But this behavior is not good. You should always be open to enhancing new knowledge and seeing/learning new things.

You may avoid the Ikea effect by:

- Get a second opinion: Asking an unbiased third party for their valuation is therefore a good way to avoid a bad valuation.
- Ask for feedback: when I used to write a chapter of this book after I am done with this, I used to tell Rohan to go through it and check stuff and he used to give a piece of true advice or suggestions on what changes to be made. And when Rohan needs any suggestions, he used to ask me. When you have worked hard on a task and it becomes difficult to stay impartial, get some trusted opinions to help broaden your outlook. This will help you with truthfulness and show you the right path. There are people who do fake appreciation, and because of that, you are unaware of the truth and mistakes. So, the truth is always better than 100 lies.

Remember not every time Ikea effect is biased. Sometimes, it is nice to value something a little more because of the effort you spend – even if that item is not seen in the same light by others. For example, there is nothing wrong with thinking your child is the smartest in the class because you are heavily invested in raising him/her.

Likewise, at times when it is useful to increase your valuation of something (such as with kids and vegetables), it's helpful to know that investing in labor may make you see things in better terms.

When you build yourself something you value it more than it should be

<u>Assignment:</u> Make a list of things which you have made with your own hard work in this 1 month whether painting, cooking or building rocket.

1.
2.
3.
4.

<u>*Goggle effect*</u>

Since Priya had a project due at school, she used Google rather than approaching her parents or another expert for advice. In this 21st century, everything is working on smartphones, which is affecting people in a terribly negative way. Yes, it is good. But when do we use it for good work?

The Google effect is the tendency to forget information that is readily available through search engines like Google. We do not commit this information to our memory because we know that this information is easy to access online.

In the past decades, people used to always remember each other's cell phone numbers or the address of the house. Let us say you are reading a book when you come across a new word. You choose to look up the word's definition on Google. A few days later, the term reappears, but you appear to have forgotten what it means.

When John and Ram met a week later and incidentally John asked, "what was that movie name which we saw a week before." "God, I just read about it yesterday, but I forgot!" Ram expressed. This is the brain that is unable to collect the information and store it as it already knows that it is available on the internet and no need to keep it safe in memory.

This effect will lose your concentration and your habit to remember anything. The recent proof of this is when we used to be small, we used to learn "Ganpati stotra", "Shiv tandav stotram" and all. But, as this all is available on google and on YouTube, it is easy to play/read from a device rather than remember in their brain.

When I used to go for the MSCIT course the students used to find the shortcuts from the goggle and use them instead of remembering and noting down in a notebook. The Google effect can make someone forget a particular keyboard shortcut they usually use if they are aware that they can quickly and readily find it online.

This bias applies to most of the information that is readily available on our computers and mobile devices, not only the stuff we look up using search engines. Do you memorize the exact address of your best friend or the number of your parents? The Google effect is to blame for the likelihood that the answer is no.

Imagine that Kaira, a young woman, loses her phone while out one night at a pub. She begins to walk home but soon realizes she is lost because she is accustomed to utilizing Google Maps. She wishes she could call a taxi or her parents to come to get her since she does not feel safe walking home alone at night. Because she always looks them up on her phone, Kaira does not know the phone numbers of any taxi companies or her parents when she encounters a pay phone. Due to her overreliance on technology, Kaira has found herself in an uncomfortable predicament from which she is unable to escape.

Imagine we seldom anticipate being in the kinds of situations where we would need to access information that we often have stored online, the Google effect can result in uncomfortable circumstances where we are unable to recall crucial information.

Before it became a threat and addiction in your life, keep it away from you. The more you focus on remembering the better it will be for you. You may read books, do meditation for calmness and revise things. These methods will surely help you.

How you can avoid this?

Challenge for you: Whenever you have to do a task, avoid the goggle, YouTube, or any other social media platform and complete the task on your own with the help of your brain or others' brain.

Pessimism bias

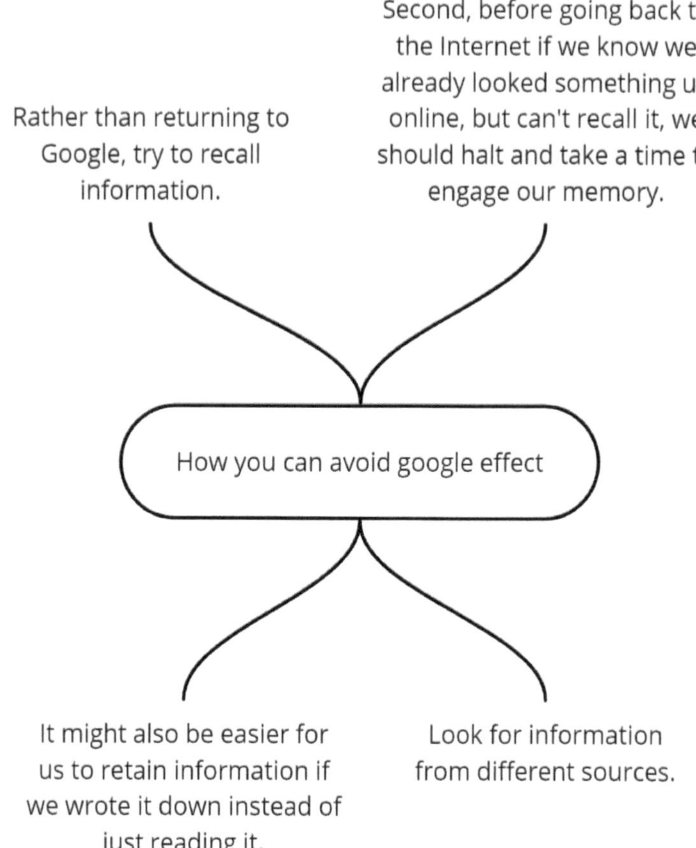

You might have thought about how your future is going to be? Will this education help in the future? Am I going to earn lakhs and billions in life? Will I be successful in the future? These questions tend to come because of the pessimism bias. It gives negative thoughts space in your brain. The pessimism bias is a cognitive bias that leads people to overestimate the chance of negative outcomes and underestimate the likelihood of happy outcomes, particularly when thinking that future events will go poorly.

Once, even after studying hard for her 12th board exam, the pessimism bias leads Kiara to feel that she will fail. She passed with good marks. Negative thoughts will come. But, when you give focus more on the positive, the negative will never arrive.

The pessimistic bias is essentially related to the propensity to overestimate how awful the future will be for you, in that you tend to overestimate the likelihood of unfavorable events and underestimate the likelihood of favorable outcomes. When I had to take the "Elementary exam" in the past, I was anxious and began to question whether I would be able to pass with good grades. Will I perform at my best? But, when I read the results after two months, I received a "B". The highest grade in the entire class. When you give space for negative thoughts, they will make the house in your mind. So, always think in a positive way and then see the changes that will happen in your life. The following are just a few problems that might result from pessimistic thinking:

- Because you believe you will not succeed, pessimism can make you avoid attempting things, for example, most students avoid giving competitive exam holding the belief in their mind that they cannot succeed.

One of my friends named Rudra attended a job interview, but the pessimism bias caused him to believe that he would probably fail the interview, despite the fact that he was qualified for the position and had performed well in previous interviews in a similar manner.

- Isha attended a party, but because of her pessimistic bias, she felt she should not approach Gabby. She assumed he would reject her, despite there being no reason for her to believe such a thought. Because of the belief that you are currently performing worse than you actually are, pessimism can make you feel more nervous.
- Being pessimistic might make you feel horrible about the past because you think that things went worse than they actually did.

The worst circumstance was not all that bad because after being rejected from the job, Raj found the best employees with a large income.

Pessimism is regarded as one of the primary signs of depression, and it is closely related to other depressive symptoms like sadness, hopelessness, and a sense of helplessness. This may be due, among other things, to the fact that depressed people frequently exhibit erratic activity in the brain regions that mediate positive emotions. The more negativity surrounds us, the more negative we become.

How can you deal with pessimism?

Pessimism has a place in both society as a whole and in our individual lives; we must have the fortitude to put up with it when its point of view is insightful. Optimism with its eyes open and flexibility rather than blind optimism is what we seek. When necessary, we must be able to draw on pessimism's strong awareness of reality, but without spending too much time in its dark holes.

Try this: *Keep a tally of negative remarks you make over the course of a week. See if you can make your daily number go down. The goal is zero.*

- **utilizing the process of thought:**

People who respond to their fear by utilizing defensive pessimism may find that thinking things through will motivate them to make the actions necessary to prevent contemplated calamity. They create many scenarios that demonstrate potential results for both good and bad, as well as multiple routes for each.

Like the way that a cognitive therapist might facilitate a patient who is anxious or depressed by pointing out unhelpful thoughts and gradually guiding the client to more adaptive ways of thinking by proposing alternatives, pointing out contradictions or overgeneralizations, and so forth, the thinking-through process serves as a way for them to acknowledge their anxieties and negativity and then cognitively work through it.

Defensive pessimists should perform better as a result since they feel better, are less anxious, and are more in control of their situation as a result. They need to feel better about their performance afterward, as a result.

In essence, the thinking-through technique is a methodical and upbeat strategy to deal with negative thoughts. To employ it, attempt to think about whatever it is you are feeling pessimistic about in a way that aids in problem-solving and if required, future planning.

For instance, if you think you are going to fail at something, consider why you think that's the case and what you can do to reduce the probability that you will fail. Consider specific scenarios that you believe could result in failure and develop responses to assist you to deal with them.

For example,

1. if you are worried about a pending job interview, you should ask yourself why you think you will fail and pinpoint the issues you feel will arise.
2. Then, in order to be better prepared, make a list of the reasons why those areas are probably going to be challenging and devise a strategy that will enable you to deal with them successfully.

What positive aspects of pessimism exist?

It is occasionally worthwhile to actively nurture a pessimistic view in yourself or others if you believe that doing so could result in a positive end. This is because positive pessimism can be helpful in some situations. Being pessimistic, for instance, may help you reduce the effects of overconfidence if you are aware that you are prone to it in a certain area and that it negatively affects your performance.

Pessimism can be developed in a variety of ways, such as by concentrating on the challenges and problems you will probably face when attending a future event. To achieve this, it is crucial to foster pessimism in a way that results in positive rather than bad outcomes.

note: -

Note in particular that you should use extreme caution when encouraging pessimism in situations were doing so can be detrimental. For instance, encouraging a person you know to be negative about the future could backfire if they lack confidence in their talents.

IX

Spirituality : A Lively Part Of Life

A belief in something greater than oneself is the wide concept of spirituality. It aims to provide answers to queries regarding the purpose of life, interpersonal relationships, universal principles, and other unsolved aspects of the human condition.

A spiritual worldview holds that there is more to existence than what people can directly experience with their senses and bodies. Instead, it implies that something more fundamental binds all living things to one another and to the cosmos as a whole.

There is no one route or set of beliefs that make up spirituality. The benefits of a spiritual encounter can be attained in a variety of ways. It depends on you how you define spirituality. For some, it is their devotion to a particular religion or their acceptance of a greater force.

Others might describe it as having a sense of interconnectedness with other people or with nature, or a sense of connection to a higher state. Among the indications of spirituality are

- serious inquiries regarding issues like suffering or what occurs after death

- strengthening interpersonal bonds
- Feeling sympathy and empathy for others
- feeling linked to everything around me
- the sensation of astonishment and amazement
- pursuing happiness independent of riches or other external benefits
- searching for purpose and meaning
- wanting to change the world for the better

Different people have different spiritual experiences and modes of expression. While some people may look for spiritual experiences in every element of their lives, others might be more inclined to feel them in particular situations or at particular places.

For instance, some people might be more prone to have spiritual experiences in temples or other places of worship, but others might experience the same emotions when out in the great outdoors.

Spirituality's various forms.

There are many different types of spirituality. Some examples of how people get in touch with their own spirituality include.

- **Breathwork**

Any kind of breathing exercise or method is referred to as breathwork. They are frequently practiced by individuals to enhance their mental, physical, and spiritual well-being. We start to connect to the truth of who we are as we begin to heal these aspects of ourselves. These powerful realizations enable us to make decisions that are more in line with our true desires than with our fears. It is the quickest method found to get out of your head, which is something most people find really difficult.

You purposefully adjust your breathing rhythm while doing breathwork. Conscious and deliberate breathing is a component of several types of breathwork therapy. Breathwork is beneficial for spiritual practice because it enables you to overcome your body and mind and connect with your inner self. Breathwork learners frequently encounter spiritual awakenings as well as the deepest levels of relaxation and meditation. Many of the difficulties that everyone faces are supported by breathwork.

- Stress is lessened,
- and openness, love,
- Peace,
- gratitude,
- clarity,
- communication, and
- connections are encouraged.

In addition to assisting with anxiety, despair, fear, grief, and rage, breathwork also aids in the release of trauma or other mental, physical, and emotional obstacles.

One of my friends, named Cristy was practicing this technique and I saw a big change in her. Cristy was a separate individual. She used to be an introvert but is now acting more like a perfectly balanced ambivert. That is a huge shift!

She is growing more at ease in her own skin.

She does not constantly occupy her thoughts. She has no fear of her feelings. Every day, she gets to know herself more. She is bringing into her life the things she has always desired despite her strong convictions that she is not deserving of them. She recognizes her value.

She cherishes herself. She is skilled at controlling her energies. She is excellent at establishing boundaries when interacting with others. She is quite clear about the things she needs and wants in life. She is also transparent when she is not! This is crucial because it enables her to recognize when she needs to center herself by going outside or practicing breathwork.

The most valuable resource you own is your breath. Your life will change if you can manipulate it to cure yourself.

- **Meditation or quiet time.**

In various religions and cultures all over the world, spiritual meditation is practiced. Others use it to calm their minds, while still others use it to reduce stress and unwind. Some still use it to awaken and strengthen their connection to something bigger than themselves. Fewer scientific research has focused on the spiritual consequences of meditation, even though several have examined how it can promote calm. This is probably because measuring spirituality is difficult.

What is spiritual meditation?

A spiritual meditation is a form of meditation that you engage in when you want to establish a connection with a higher power, such as God, the universe, your Higher Self, etc.

Spiritual meditation focuses on strengthening one's connection to a higher power and understanding spiritual/religious meaning.

Spiritual meditation, in contrast to other types, focuses on more than just stress relief or relaxation.

Spiritual benefits of meditation.

- greater inner serenity and peace, less reactivity, and a more balanced sense of self
- a blissful state of being inside oneself that is independent of external conditions
- a deep, true understanding of who you are at your soul level, less unhealthy stress, and more creativity
- Increased self-esteem, self-trust, and self-acceptance are results of a strong sense of belonging.
- your life's mission is crystal clear.

Here are the three 10-minute sections of your daily meditation/ quite time that can get you started:

-The first three 10-minute

segments of your daily meditation session are listed below.

the initial ten minutes

There are two steps to entering a state of spiritual concentration and meditation:

Pray, and let go of any worries that are keeping you from God.

Read a scripture three times to help you focus your mind completely on God.

Because of what you did during the first 10 minutes of your meditation time, this portion of it should be "silent." You need to relax your thoughts. Yes, it is possible to go ten minutes without looking at your smartphone notifications or attempting to control something that is naturally uncontrollable. Just ten minutes remain!

, "Express my emotions.": Pray to recognize your dominating positive and negative feelings as you say.

Confess your guilt - Ask God to show you the sins that are causing your guilt to cloud or divert your thoughts.

The final 10 minutes, in the end,

The last 10 minutes are all about reading and applying Scripture.

Develop or Maintain Your Plan - Read scripture that directs and inspires you to stick with your strategy for improving yourself, your life, or the lives of others.

Send in your requests - Ask God for just what you need to advance your plan.

The 30-minute Quiet Time is a starting point for meditation. It allows you to get back in touch with God by centering your thoughts and emotions on him. Additionally, it aids in maintaining your attention on the goals God has placed in your heart so you can move closer every day to realizing those aspirations.

Try it for seven days if you want. How much it changes your life will astonish you!

- **Prayer.**

All relationships are built on communication. And the way in which we communicate with our creator is through prayer. The Atama and the Paramatma are connected through spirituality. This relationship is strengthened by prayer and meditation. Our relationship with God is founded on faith and spirituality, just as relationships are built on trust and love. Our instinct, intuition, insight, and foresight are tremendously sharpened by having a strong faith in God, practicing regular prayer, and engaging in meditation; it is almost as if we're letting the supreme force run our lives in this way. Because of the established link, when spiritual people look for solutions, they can be sure to discover them in some signs from the universe in the most surprising circumstances. Chanting is a spiritual practice that, when done correctly, produces wonderful vibrations.

Once, a mom received a phone call while at work informing her that her young daughter was severely ill and running a fever. She left her job and went to the drugstore to pick up some prescription medication. When she returned to her car, she discovered that she had left her keys inside. She contacted her home and informed the babysitter of the situation because she was unsure of what to do. She was informed by the babysitter that her temperature was worsening. You could use a coat hanger to open the door, she said.

When the woman turned to look around, she discovered an old, rusted coat hanger that had been dropped on the ground, possibly by someone else who had once locked their car keys within. "I don't know how to use this," she stated as she had a glance at the hanger. She requested God in prayer to send her assistance.

Within five minutes, an ancient, beat-up motorcycle with a dirty, bearded man riding it and donning an old biker skull rag on his helmet pulled up.

"This is what you brought to help me?" the woman wondered. But. because of her desperation, she simply remained silent. The man inquired whether he could help as he dismounted from his bicycle. "Yes, my kid is extremely ill," she acknowledged. "I pulled over to give her some medicine, but I forgot my keys in the car. I had to bring her home. Please, could you unlock my car with this hanger?"

"Sure," he replied. When he approached the automobile, it had already been opened for less than a minute.

Through her emotions, she expressed her gratitude to the man and added, "Thank you so much! You are a wonderful man."

"I'm not a kind man, lady," the man said in response. I recently been released from prison. I was incarcerated for auto theft and have only been released briefly.

She expressed gratitude to the man once more and yelled aloud, "Oh, Thank God! You even sent me a qualified individual!

Maintain your faith in God, pray to Him, and exercise patience. He will assist us in ways we never could have anticipated.

- **Spending time in nature**

Nature has the capacity to be endowed with spiritual significance and force. Mountains, lakes, and forests can evoke awe or a sense of the holy. They are tools that people can use to establish spiritual connections and elicit spiritual experiences. The first level of experience we have is the most crucial since it involves our relationship with the environment. All the various layers of our existence benefit when our environment is healthy and good. They finally find equilibrium as a result, and we feel more at ease and connected to both the people around us and ourselves. It has a beneficial effect on all the other layers of our existence if our environment is healthy and cheerful. In doing so, they are brought into harmony, and as a result, we feel more at ease and connected to both the people around us and ourselves.

spiritual advantages of surrounding yourself with natural beauty.

- Engage all your senses:

In nature, we are exposed to sights, sounds, scents, and tastes that are different from those we encounter every day. This allows us to use all of our senses and links the mind and body. The energy that flows through ourselves and through plants, trees, and animals is the same energy that flows across the entire cosmos. Interacting with the vital force that permeates everything of nature strengthens us and uplifts our spirits.

- Recognize the finite:

Looking at nature also serves as a reminder of our transience; we are born into this planet and will return to it, leaving our minds and energies behind to continue the cosmos' journey.

- Find out who you really are:

Spending time outside reveals aspects of your personality with which you have lost touch. You become aware of your true self and learn to accept who you are.

- Discover the divine:

Connecting with nature reveals the divine to us. Everything around you reflect it, from the size of the area to the tiniest features in the nearby plants, flowers, and insects.

Humans and nature have had a special spiritual connection since the beginning of time. She serves as our model mother. She is in us, and we are in her. Ayurveda advises us to spend as much time as we can outside, admiring nature, and taking time for introspection.

- Yoga

A successful yoga practice enables its practitioners to find peace, both inside themselves and with the environment they live in. Yoga's spiritual practice places less emphasis on posture perfection and more on achieving inner calm and clarity. Yoga is a form of spiritual practice that strives to unite the individual soul, or Atama—a portion of God that resides inside the human body—with Param Atama, or the Supreme Self, also known as Brahman, the unmanifested God without a second. This is based on Lord Krishna's statement in the Bhagavad Gita that "I am situated in the hearts of all."

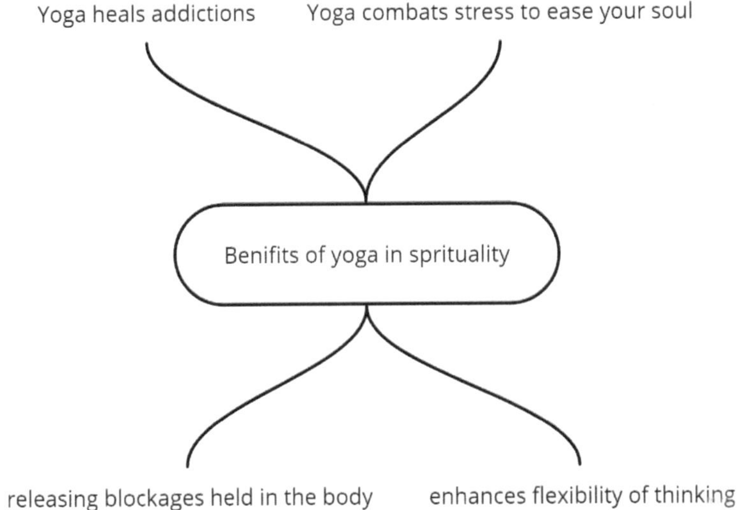

X

Tools To Become UNSTOPPABLE

This chapter is very straightforward and consists of tools that will help you follow the rituals and activities that the authors talk about in the book.

The correct method to make affirmations

You will undoubtedly be familiar with this tool and how to apply it if you participate in webinars or watch motivational videos on YouTube. Still, today you will discover a new technique for affirmations. Affirmations are essentially statements of truth that we repeat aloud to ourselves regularly to change our negative thought patterns. The way you talk to yourself counts, whether you are feeling euphoric after making a significant achievement or depressed after having a difficult day. Affirmations are short statements that you can repeat to alter your thoughts and feelings about yourself. Affirmations are frequently used in conjunction with meditation and yoga, so you may already be familiar with them if you engage in these activities. People frequently do this blunder while making affirmations such as *"I am going to be successful"* or *"I am going to make money."* Making affirmations in this manner is incorrect.

Recently I attended a webinar on the law of attraction. And it was stated that you should never make affirmations regarding the future or how your future will be. Whenever you make it by using the present tense like that thing is happening with you in present. For example, *"I am successful"* or *"I am a billionaire."*

Positive discourse attracts positive things, and the same holds for you when you talk to yourself with an upbeat mindset. Early when I heard about this method, I too made the same mistake of writing it in the future tense but I don't want you to do this same mistake! and Work on this. When I was 16th years old, I used to see some videos regarding motivational topics or how to make money and I saw the life-changing seminar of sir SANDEEP MAHESHWARI you would be knowing him he is a motivational speaker and an entrepreneur too. So, he gave affirmations to his audience which I read but I wanted to make mine which has the power of making

This is the way you make it: "AIIAH"- "As-if-I-already-have" whenever you make affirmation always assume and set that thing in your mind that I already have it. Like if you want to buy a house you may say "*I am living in a big bungalow*"

And it works. When your focus goes on positive things that thing will eventually happen in your life.

How can you make affirmations?

- Specific end result: - when you make an affirmation keep it in mind and make the affirmation accordingly to it like what you want to achieve or what your focus is. Like, for example, if I want to be an artist then the affirmation will be "I *am a successful artist and earning a lot of capital*".
- As if its already done: - when you think that you have already achieved the goals then it gets fixed into your subconscious mind and your mind starts to believe it and then gradually that things

happen "I am studying in my dream university" and see the result it will come true.

- Add emotions:-I informed you in the previous sentence that I did not apply the affirmations offered by Sir SANDEEP MAHESHWARI. The only explanation for this is that when you create your own affirmations, they also include your desires, goals, and emotions. When you include your feelings when creating it, you feel more connected to yourself, and when you repeat it each morning and evening, you feel the same way. Include the emotional words like happy, delighted, feeling rich, surprised, and amazed in your affirmation sentences to feel the goal that you wrote and assuming as completed.
- Create happiness and say: - maintain a smile With a smile, everyone's face looks fantastic. When you speak to yourself and make affirmations, smile broadly as you do so. You will feel pleased and good about this. and will always keep you aware.

If you have not done so already, after finishing the book, be sure to say your personal affirmations twice, preferably in the morning and at night. When you read an affirmation in the morning, your day starts out new and you stay optimistic all day. Additionally, after reading the affirmations at night, you feel satisfied and drift off to sleep with your goals in your mind.

I am going to be succesfull i am going to earn a lot Iam going to stay healthy I am going to stay happyy	I am delighet and fulfilled to be successful" I am proud to Earn 1 crore in 3 months and satisfied I am Healthy and Joyful I am Happyy and enjoying life.

Gratitude: truly living in the present

Living in present has got a huge hype over the past few years. As the public is becoming more aware of health and inclining towards spirituality, the statement "Live in present" is on the top of every tongue. Some say, concentrate on your breath and you will live in present. Some suggest meditating and focusing on stomach movement. However, all this focus comes to an end when we see the scripture that are widely followed by yogis in their sadhanas. One such famous scripture is "Vigyan Bhairav Tantra." This scripture is said to be spoken by lord shiva himself. The absence of any random motivation and suggestion makes this book my favorite. It has pure practical knowledge of various sadhanas whose effects highlight directly on our body and in life. Well, in this Lord Shiva says to concentrate and acknowledge the pause between exhalation and inhalation. When a human turns from breath into breath out, there is a tiny time period where we stop before the transition. Also, when we voluntarily stop our breath, do we die? Don't we still realize and address the moment we are in? We do. This proves that breathing is a metabolism like all other in our body. So, what is living in present?

We must understand that **"we have nothing until we acknowledge something."** I do not have a mother until I say that I have one or address and feel her presence or go and talk to her or just see a lady and remind myself that she is my mother. Thus, acknowledgement is the kye. And the best way to acknowledge is gratitude. Saying "Thank you" and feeling grateful for someone or something connects you to that person or thing. This connection lets you feel the timeline of that object and a bliss inside you. At present everything around you is present. They all are in existence.

Recall the times where you remember your past and according to the weight of the memory you cry or smile. So, that past is at present for you because in present you are acknowledging the thing which was sometime before past for you. Similarly, when you acknowledge and be grateful for now, you live in the present. That is the reason GIVER ritual that you learned in the previous chapter is so important. 'G' for Gratitude.

In conclusion, living in present has nothing necessarily to do with the breath, it depends on your awareness, observation, and acknowledgement of the surrounding things.

The secret of magic of water.

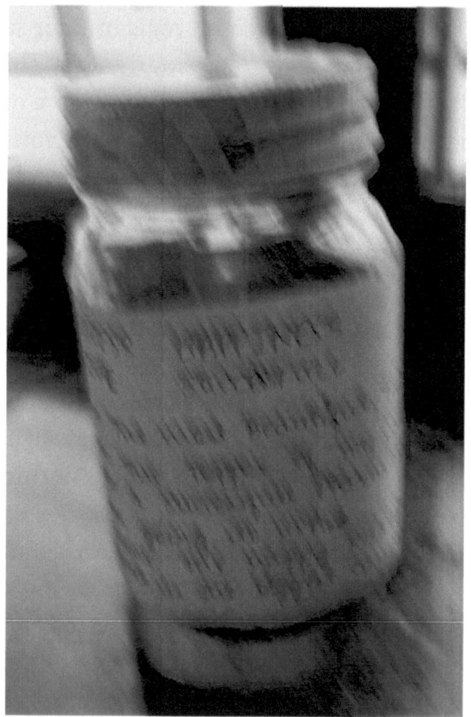

Enter Caption

As you can see in the photo up above, which features a glass bottle and a paper stick with writing on it, what do you think what's on it? Umm.. guess. I will now explain how this magic trick transformed my life. c'mon, let us go further.

Have you ever heard about this magic water and how can it make changes in your life? So basically, magic is made by Writing your goals and affirmations down on paper and reciting them to a glass or bottle of water is an intriguing practice.

Your objectives and affirmations will eventually come true if you use this strategy to write them down and then stick with them. It is based on the idea that water has specific healing capabilities and is a potent energy-information conductor.

Here is an experiment you need to conduct,

Take two glasses, fill them with the same quantity of water, and affix the papers with the words "Love" on the first glass and "Hate" on the second.

When you retrieve it later, you can observe the changes that have occurred after a few hours in the refrigerator.

When you see a glass of water that is transformed into "love," the ice has a good shape, but when you see a glass of water that is transformed into "hate," the ice is broken and has the wrong shape. Why must this occur? Love attracts good since it has a positive energy, while hate attracts bad energy, negative vibrations, and negative ideas, which is why the ice lost its crystalline shape.

Like this, it is believed that when water is surrounded by positive energy, it will eventually enter us when we drink that water and what we desire will take place. It is one of the manifestation techniques.

How to use it?

1. Grab a glass cup or bottle.
2. Take a paper, and on it, specifically write down your objectives and affirmation.
3. Activate the energy flow in your hands by rubbing your palms together and then hold the glass/bottle.
4. Attach that paper to the glass bottle or cup and write on it (what you want in life or your yearly goal).
5. Fill the glass with water before going to bed and leave it there all night.
6. Visualize what you are saying and repeat until and unless you feel that energy in you.
7. Drink it the following morning when you awaken, or you can sip on it throughout the day.

When you see in morning it will have little bubbles on it. Try not to reveal your magic affirmations or goals because it is thought that doing so will weaken them and decrease your chances of success.

WHY THIS CAUSES THE WATER MANIFESTATION TECHNIQUE TO FAIL OR NOT WORK FOR YOU

You must have a thorough understanding of the laws or concepts before using this worldwide secret source to create your desires using water. Your cells' and tissues' water content were the only factor in the change.

- You should not be angry because of this.
- Not being frustrated is appropriate.
- You should not be depressed.

At that point, your energy declines because your body's water particles have less energy. So perform this technique with lot of good vibrations and with having focus in your life.

Wim-Hof breathing + cold shower

Wim-Hof breathwork is an intense meditative breathing technic that has the ability to calm any cluttered mind and take you into a trans immediately. The technic's potential and ability to give quick result is what made it world famous. The breath work takes 30 minutes to take you in another dimension. However, it also needs good strong lungs as at later stages you need to hold the breath even for 3 minutes and more. It sounds crazy for a normal human being, but this is possible as I too have done it. But, it is difficult for some people to hold the breaths for the allotted time. Hence, I modified it by adding one step. This method is tested and works completely perfect in the favor of those who cannot hold the breath for a long time. Later, you will be experienced and able to hold it for a longer time.

Let us start! Here is how Wim Hof breathing is done.

Deeply breath in and breath out completely. Suck in your stomach as much as possible breath out fully. Breath in fully, again. Breath out. Repeat this breath in breath out for 30 - 40 times. Now perform the 40th breath in, breath out fully and stop. Hold your breath outside your body for 1 minute. After one minute is over, breath in fully and hold for 15 minutes. Meanwhile, tap hard on your stomach near belly, then on your neck near Adam's apple, and on your chest in order. Finally, let the breath fully out. **This is the first round complete.**

Now, repeat the breathing pattern in the second round, but hold for 1 minute 30 seconds. In the third round, repeat the breathing and hold for 2 minutes. With every round increase the time to hold your breath out of the body by 30 seconds. The time to hold your breath in and tapping on stomach, neck, and chest will stay the same in every round that is 15 seconds.

Now, in the end round, whatever may be your last round; Do everything the same. But, this time, tap on your crown chakra before releasing the hold-in breath. Now, sit quietly and feel the effect. Note that all that is happening is because the change in the body metabolism and there is nothing to worry. I usually do four to five rounds of this breathing and I would recommend it too. If you are willing to take it ahead to the extreme, then kindly see a doctor and take advise before continuing. You might not listen any sound from the outside world and only sound will be that of crickets in your ears. That is totally normal. You even might get current flowing through your body and tingling sensation. This all means that energy is flowing through your body as you just tapped in the try for chakra activation. You just have to sit quiet, close your eyes, and acknowledge all these affects you feel.

Remember:

- For beginners, breath in through the nose and mouth both. Let both open and breath in fully. Later, after spending considerable time with Wim-Hof breathing method, use only nose to breath in.
- For breathing out, strictly use only mouth.
- Now, pronounce the letter 'O.' did you observed the shape of your mouth opening? While breathing in or out through mouth, the shape of mouth should be in this state. Here, when you breath out your chicks pump out and while breathing in and out a sound occurs.
- The force that you use in breathing in and out in a given time too defines the benefits you feel. So, do not do this too slow or too fast do it little faster where you will have to force your breath in and out, but you also feel it moving in and out and making you calmer.
- While tapping, tap harder. Tapping should not hurt you but it should make you feel tap to free up your energy blockages. Tapping has no specific number. You may tap until you feel like you really tapped. I tap with a little higher force for 3 to 5 times

on each place and gently for 3 to 5 time on crown chakra.

- This breathing can be done laying down or siting up in a comfortable position where your stomach can move freely, and you do not feel any strain in any of your body part.
- Do not practice this breathing while doing any work that needs complete conscious attention like driving, working with factory machinery or so. The breathing has the power to make you fall asleep or take you to a trans where you become a little unconscious about your surroundings. So, take these precautions.
- The people who are unable to hold the breath until the time ends should breath fully in, fully out, then stop again until you feel the urge to breath or time ends. If the urges feels again, then repeat the same method- one time breath.

To end up this breathing part, I would like to talk about the cold shower. Not benefits as I want you to be experimental. But, on a recommendation, I would suggest you all to take cold shower and embrace the pain every morning. It gets you complete out of that sleepy state and make the energy flow through your body to get you ready for a productive day ahead. You will even feel current running through your body while in cold shower. Before taking a cold shower, wet your head first. If not fully then at least put some drops on head and on your crown chakra so that you head feels cool. Then, you may start with your bath. **Not wetting your head and making it feel at low temperature before bathing with cold water can be deadly. If not done, then heat can directly shoot towards your brain from the body and destroy the cells. So, it is better to wet the head and absorb the heat in the rest of the body.**

You may find the guided Wim-Hof breathing on YouTube as well. I follow it from the channel named- “Medit-o-rama.” You may use this guided in the beginning.

The daily two or three doses of Wim-Hof breathing with a cold shower in the morning after exercise and breathing benefits on a large scale in long term. Throughout the book we wrote about specific benefits of the practices. For this topic, there will be no benefits. Wim-Hof breathing is special and I recommend you do it to see the benefits yourself.

CONGRATULATIONS

We are grateful to you readers for giving your time towards your self-development. We hope to see you on the upgraded level of your life. All the best with your self-development journey. Do not hesitate to share your reviews and connect to authors on social media personally. Share your thoughts and enquire if you have problems in your self-development journey.

Stay tuned for our next interesting and productive book.

THANK YOU

www.ingramcontent.com/pod-product-compliance
Ingram Content Group UK Ltd.
Pitfield, Milton Keynes, MK11 3LW, UK
UKHW041824200726
13854UKWH00002BA/554